SPECTACULAR FLOWERS

SPECTACULAR FLOWERS

Diana Tonks

with a foreword by Lord Lichfield

B T BATSFORD LTD LONDON

ACKNOWLEDGEMENTS

ARBURY HALL, The Right Hon. The Viscount and Viscountess Daventry.

BLENHEIM PALACE, His Grace the Duke of Marlborough.

CASTLE HOWARD, The Hon. Mrs Simon Howard.

GLAMIS CASTLE, Mary Countess of Strathmore and Kinghorne/Strathmore Estates (Holdings) Ltd.

HAGLEY HALL, The Right Hon. The Viscount and Viscountess Cobham.

HANCH HALL, Mr and Mrs Douglas Milton-Haynes.

HOLME PIERREPONT HALL, Mr and Mrs Robin Brackenbury.

KEDLESTON HALL, The Right Hon. The Viscountess Scarsdale, and The National Trust, who took over the property in March 1987.

RAGLEY HALL, The Marquess and Marchioness of Hertford.

ROCKINGHAM CASTLE, Commander and Mrs L. M. M. Saunders Watson, DL.

SHUGBOROUGH, Shugborough Estate, a National Trust Property, financed and administered by Staffordshire County Council, and The Right Hon. The Earl of Lichfield.

STANFORD HALL, The Lady Braye.

STONELEIGH ABBEY, The Right Hon. The Lord and Lady Leigh.

WARWICK CASTLE, by kind permission of Warwick Castle.

WESTON PARK, The Weston Park Foundation.

For the photography, Stewart Downie for all illustrations except the following: Castle Howard, by courtesy of the Hon. Simon Howard (page 32); Derick Bonsall (ARPS) for arrangements, courtesy of *The Flower Arranger* (pages 36 and 37); Woodmansterne Ltd for Glamis in the spring (page 40); Barrie Taylor (FRPS) for Blenheim Palace (pages 29, 30 and 31); and Jeremy Whitaker (MSIA) for Blenheim Palace (pages 26 and 27).

For helping with plant identification, Daphne Vagg and Ann Smith at Geo H Smith Nurseries Ltd.

For kindly providing the dried arrangements at Glamis, Yvonne Mallet.

For assisting with photography and editorial queries, Paul Duffie (FTS), the administrator at Blenheim Palace.

For individual help and support, Chris and Lisa Tonks, Stanley and Daphne Dodds, Nicola Evans, all my family and friends, my assistant, Kay Railton, who helped with all the arrangements at the stately homes, the staff of Diana of Boldmere, and Pat Day of *Day One* for her initial encouragement.

For my family

First published 1991

© Diana Tonks

ISBN 0 7134 6552 2

Printed in Hong Kong
for the publishers
B T Batsford Ltd
4 Fitzhardinge Street
London W1H 0AH

CONTENTS

FOREWORD

by Lord Lichfield

Spectacular Flowers is a book that I believe will bring pleasure to anyone who enjoys the beauty of the traditional room and the natural colour and vibrancy that flowers add to it. Yet this is not only a book for flower arrangers or those who simply love flowers. It will also offer a great deal to anyone who appreciates interior design and architectural heritage, as the settings are some of the most sumptuous examples of stately and historic homes in Britain.

From a purely photographic point of view, the locations are stunning, each captured by the eye of the camera with meticulous precision and an admirable artistry. The mediaeval stone walls of Warwick Castle and the formal splendours of Blenheim Palace – to take two examples – afford magnificent backdrops for arrangements and exemplify British heritage in all its distinction, individuality and grandeur.

As for the flowers, they range from the unashamedly extravagant to the simple but splendid. The former are designed to inspire you for the most spectacular occasion: a family wedding, a Christening or a harvest supper, for instance. Others that are simpler and easier to put together will still hold any visitor's eye as he or she walks into the room for the first time.

Thus, this is not just a dream book. The flower arrangements have all been chosen with the same considerations that any arranger would apply. How the flowers can blend and enhance the colours of the room, how foliage can be used to lengthen and lighten an arrangement, or how flowers can be made to last and look their best in a heated environment.

Practicalities that would affect any home setting are tackled with the professional eye of Diana Tonks, a florist who understands the inseparability of flowers from beautiful interiors and applies a perfectionist vigour to her art. She treats flower arranging as essential decoration, which brings pleasure to both the artist and the viewer.

Finally, I think it is important to add that all of the homes featured in the book are open to the public and that they will benefit and survive through your support. Enjoy *Spectacular Flowers* as a reminder of the architectural heritage of Britain that is still accessible today, and as a remarkable and luxurious tribute to flowers in your home, as well as mine.

THE RIGHT HON. THE EARL OF LICHFIELD

INTRODUCTION

For hundreds of years, flowers have been picked for the home, bringing some of the beauty of the outdoors to the inside. Originally, flowers tended to be placed naturally in a vase or jug, or arranged in a favourite container. Flower arranging as a formal art did not really begin until Georgian times, later developing under Queen Victoria and becoming an established part of interior decoration today.

COLOURS

In the homes featured in this book, flowers play an intrinsic part – in the tapestries, the paintings and the furniture. Not everyone will be faced with such lavish settings when they try arranging, and such an abundance of decoration can make the flower arranger's job very difficult. In nearly all my arrangements, I opted for contrasting or complementary colours rather than attempting to match exactly the opulent surrounding decor.

You may also want to bring a warmth or coolness to your room with flowers. Moods, seasons, and ideas can all be suggested with different colours and the language of flowers is richly evocative. The reds, oranges and yellows at the hot end of the spectrum can convey joy, strength and summer. The cooler side of the spectrum, with the lilacs, blues, mauves and purples are receding colours that blend together easily, and suggest coolness, tranquility and purity. And then, of course, there is green; foliage introduces a necessary neutral balance that has a stabilizing influence in your design, separating flowers and making blooms more colourful by its presence. Green suggests life and will always add a freshness and vitality to your design.

Although there are many theories on colour in flower arranging, do not be afraid to experiment. Spend some time studying a colour wheel to see how well shades harmonize. You could perhaps try arrangements of complementary colours – those that lie opposite each other on the colour wheel and offer a contrast; or of analogous colours – those that are next to each other on a colour wheel and blend together. In any event, choose what is pleasing to the eye and looks as though it were made for the room.

CONTAINERS

All the houses featured in this book are filled with priceless antiques, including vases, jugs, bowls and containers of all shapes and sizes. In a number of venues, I was allowed to use containers that belonged to the house, which enhanced the setting and personalized the arrangement. Where it was not possible, I substituted a simple dish or bowl which did not intrude and could be concealed by flowers and foliage if necessary.

In such vivid surroundings, a colourful vase filled with flowers is often too fussy anyway. It is often better to keep flowers in context; present a subtle effect rather than overstate and spoil a tastefully designed floral piece. Choose containers that will enhance all your material and not detract from its colours. Blacks, beiges, whites, stones, and greys are all suitable and will not draw the eye away from the flowers. Alternatively, a splendid piece of china or glass may well inspire you to create a beautiful arrangement, or you could use it as the centrepiece itself.

CONDITIONING AND CARE

Stately homes have traditionally prided themselves on the flowers grown in their gardens. Blooms cultivated by the head gardener were proudly brought into the house to be enjoyed by the family. Today, little has changed except that fee-paying visitors have given the family's flowers another audience. Flowers arranged for the public are often done by the owners of the homes, and I have included a selection of their ideas and approaches to arrangements that gives an interesting insight into the way the homes are decorated today.

If you have your own flower garden, always pick your plant material in the cool part of the day – morning is best. It is advisable to leave it in a cool place for several hours to have a good drink. Roses need quite a deep bucket of water, so the flowers get a really good drink before being arranged. First, strip off the unwanted foliage, removing any leaves which are below the water-line. It is important to eliminate the cause of bacteria in the water as the decaying properties will shorten the life of your flowers. To do this, the water should be fresh and topped up regularly. It is suggested nowadays that to reduce the bacteria build-up we should cut each stem, including woody, at a slanting angle instead of hammering the ends.

Although not everyone is lucky enough to have a garden or a greenhouse that can yield the types of hot-house blooms required in the most spectacular of arrangements, florists will always be at hand to satisfy most people's needs. Flowers need to be purchased from a good quality shop if you really want them to last and remain fresh for as long as possible. When your choice is made, carefully transport them home. Ideally buy them the day before required, so ensuring that they have a good long drink in a cool room before you handle them again. Remember to re-cut the stems of each flower, re-opening their sealed ends, then plunge them into a deep bucket of cool water overnight. Your flowers then have time to recover from their long journey, as many will have travelled hundreds of miles by air before gracing our living rooms.

Large chrysanthemum blooms in particular can often be off-putting because of their size and delicate structure. It is so easy to shatter a bloom by being too heavy handed. Treat them gently and as long as you handle them with care you should have no problem. It is best to have the flowers for each arrangement standing in a bucket containing a little water as it is easy to see your flower selection at a glance. Each flower also stands separately and by working in this way you reduce the risk of bruising. If you lay your flowers out on a work surface, frequent handling can easily damage your blooms.

Each night remove your arrangement from its position of display, into the kitchen or laundry area. Fill your container with fresh clean water; your flowers do not drink all the water themselves but with central heating a great deal will evaporate into the atmosphere so a little top spraying is also recommended at this stage. Leave them in a cool place overnight and put them back on display in the morning looking fresh and beautiful, ready to be admired for another day.

CHOOSING AN ARRANGEMENT AND A LOCATION

A good position for flowers is paramount for successful decoration. Always look at the room as a whole, taking into consideration the lighting, including natural light available through open windows. Take note of where furniture is placed and then decide where your flower arrangement would be seen to its best advantage. Choose a position where your display can be viewed prominently and not be hidden by a chair or a piece of furniture. Never use the television as a base for your arrangement it is often quite tempting to do so but apart from water being dangerous near electricity, your flowers will have a very short life span as a television gives off a tremendous amount of heat.

You may decide to brighten a dark and dull corner, or if the fireplace is not in use, choose to display something in the empty grate. The style of your display will be determined by how a room has been fashioned, and I have attempted to show my reasons for choosing a particular style, bloom or colour as a result of the surrounding furnishings.

If you are planning to arrange flowers in a special setting – a church, hotel, cathedral or marquee – it is a good idea to visit the location several times first.

I made at least one visit, and in some cases a number of visits, to all these houses before a flower was touched or style even thought of. It was important to discover the atmosphere of each of these great buildings. Some contain small, modest rooms, others huge ballrooms of immense proportions. In either case, the same principle applied – that of using flowers to *complement* individual settings, rather than detract from them. Beautiful flowers can enhance any room setting and bring it to life.

I have given you help in preparing your floral displays, but tried not to repeat the instruction procedure too often. The flower guide listed by each arrangement should be useful, and with many of the displays there are suggestions for tailoring the arrangements for particular celebrations, from an Easter morning, to a wedding pedestal, to a pot-et-fleur, to an autumn banquet to a Christmas party, the choice is yours!

ARBURY HALL

This magnificent Elizabethan house in Warwickshire was gothicized during the eighteenth century and has been the home of the Newdigate family since 1586. Today the house is probably one of the best preserved gothic buildings in Britain, and it can make the unusual boast of having a stable-block door designed by Sir Christopher Wren.

Arbury Hall has connections with the famous novelist George Eliot; *Mr Gilfil's Love Story* from *Scenes of Clerical Life* was based on Arbury Hall, with Sir Roger Newdigate portrayed as Sir Christopher Cheverel. George Eliot, who was christened

The Hall, Arbury Hall

Mary Ann, was born in 1819, and at the time of her birth her father, Robert, Evans was the estate bailiff at Arbury.

THE HALL

Entering the house through the hall, you experience your first taste of the extraordinary gothic interior; behind each door lies a hidden surprise. There is a wealth of intricately decorated ceilings and plasterwork resembling the delicate icing on some magnificent wedding cake. A portrait by Arthur Devis of Sir Roger Newdigate, probably painted in 1756, stands beneath the sweeping stairway.

GRACIOUS LIVING

Here is a fresh selection of summer flowers, including gladioli, carnations, sweet peas and chrysanthemum 'Penny Lane'.

The Solomon's seal used here comes just as it is picked. Quite often the foliage is stripped off, leaving just the tiny bell-shaped flowers on their stem, but it looks wonderful left whole. Giant antirrhinums add strength, both in colour and shape, to this design, which is displayed on a superb, old pedestal-container belonging to Arbury Hall. The three-legged stand has been used many times over the years and creates an equally attractive display with a varied selection of house plants. This design itself was

FLOWERS

Gladiolus 'Friendship' (sword lily)

Dianthus (perpetual-flowering carnation)

Antirrhinum majus (snapdragon)

Dianthus (spray carnation)

Lathyrus odoratus (sweet pea)

Chrysanthemum 'Penny Lane'

FOLIAGE

Lonicera (honeysuckle)

Ruscus hypophyllum

Melaleuca

Eucalyptus (gum tree)

Polygonatum (Solomon's seal)

Tsuga (western hemlock or sugar pine)

Weigela

The Little Sitting Room, Arbury Hall

inspired by the picture of Sir Roger Newdigate, and the floral display follows the lines of his stance.

Flowers of varying shapes and sizes cascade quite naturally downwards, creating an impressive display. The strong red forms a link with the deep red carpet and pink softens the overall colouring in the room.

THE LITTLE SITTING ROOM

An arched window spreads sunlight along the contours of the groined ceiling and across the room. The gothic, decorated ceiling dates back to about 1740, and the original sketch for its design was found amongst the Newdigate papers. Most of the paintings are family portraits and the large painting on the panelling above the fireplace depicts the life of Sir John de Astley, a fifteenth-century ancestor.

SUNSHINE AND SKY

A simple bowl arrangement created in a base of floral foam, using deep blue irises, yellow carnations, cream lilies and cream sweet peas. The blue irises link with the similarly coloured china on display in the cabinet beyond and create a unity within the room. Irises have quite a definite form; each flower is divided up into three sections of petals. They are effective mixed with other flowers, or can stand simply on their own in a water arrangement. Preferring a position in full sunlight, they can be grown quite easily in the garden. This variety has a strong yellow vein marking on the outer petals, which matches the yellow, cream and buttermilk in the surrounding flowers. The spiky variegated phormium leaves form a definite line to the right of the display, and by using the sweet peas and spray carnations gentle movement is added to soften an otherwise severe design.

THE SALOON

This room, which is situated at the east front of the house, is lit by a vast bow window, and, in the evening, by a splendid, glittering chandelier. Overwhelming the room completely is the elaborate gothic ceiling, full of intricate details. There are paintings of Sir Roger Newdigate and his second wife and another of St John the Baptist by Sir Joshua Reynolds. The magnificent grand piano near the window provides a definite focal point in the room.

FLOWERS
Iris 'Ideal' (iris)
Dianthus (perpetual-flowering carnation)
Lilium 'Mont Blanc' (lily)
Cream *Dianthus* (spray carnation)
Lathyrus odoratus (sweet pea)

FOLIAGE
Phormium tenax 'Variegatum'
Euphorbia polychroma
Mentha rotundifolia 'Apple Mint'
Hosta
Euonymus japonica 'Ovatus Aureus'
Rosmarinus officinalis (rosemary)
Arachniodes adiantiformis (leather fern)

The Saloon, Arbury Hall

FLOWERS

Gladiolus 'White Friendship' (sword lily)

Lilium 'Mont Blanc'

Dianthus 'Red Baron' (spray carnation)

Antirrhinum majus (snapdragon)

Matthiola incana (stock/gilliflower)

Chrysanthemum 'Lilac Byoux'

Convallaria majalis (lily-of-the-valley)

Dianthus (perpetual-flowering carnation)

Dendrobium orchidaceae

Tellima grandiflora

FOLIAGE

Choisya ternata (Mexican orange)

Polygonatum (Solomon's seal)

Lonicera (honeysuckle)

Weigela

Cineraria maritima 'Silver Dust'

Apple blossom

Skimmia japonica

PINK PERFECTION

The grand piano is a wonderful foil for flowers. As you stand in wonder looking at the immense plasterwork, your eyes are suddenly caught by the arrangement on the dark wood. This is a deceivingly large floral piece with its giant antirrhinums alongside gladioli curving upwards, giving height to this 4-foot pyramid. Shades of pink include stocks, spray chrysanthemums 'Lilac Byoux', vibrant mauve dendrobium orchids ('Madame Pompadour') and additional cream gladioli and lilies that echo the surrounding wall colouring. This raised container belonging to Viscountess Daventry, is often used to display flowers at Arbury Hall. The design is sectioned by carnations flowing to the right and by orchids to the left, and yet still maintains a balanced structure. The naturally curved pieces of Solomon's seal and *Tellima grandiflora* with their little bell-like flowers create a graceful line. The red is echoed by the edging on the photograph frame and can be found again in the carpet.

19

THE DINING ROOM

The dining room occupies the site of the hall area in the original Elizabethan house and shows off the great height of the fan-vaulted ceiling. A selection of classical statues displayed in niches decorate the wall, along with numerous Elizabethan and Jacobean portraits, including one by John Bettes of Queen Elizabeth I.

AN ELEGANT CENTREPIECE

Once again, the delicate combination of pink and cream flowers surrounded by silver and crystal hints at a gracious life style. The heavy silver container has a deep bowl and is ideal for flowers as there is enough space for topping up with water daily.

This delightful dining-table centrepiece incorporates soft pastel colours with a subtle fragrance. As the display is going to be viewed from close quarters, it is important to select flowers that blend well together; their perfume is an added bonus. Red has a strong presence in this room; pink and lilacs make a subtle change and are seen here in light relief. The more solid rose buds are interspersed with delicate lily-of-the-valley and frilly chrysanthemum 'Lilac Byoux' to soften the outline.

The Dining Room, Arbury Hall

FLOWERS
Freesia 'Blue Heaven'

Rosa veronica (pink rose)

Lathyrus odoratus (sweet pea)

Chrysanthemum 'Lilac Byoux'

Dendrobium (Singapore orchid)

Aquilegia vulgaris (Granny's bonnet)

Convallaria majalis (lily-of-the-valley)

FOLIAGE
Lonicera (honeysuckle)

Melaleuca

Nephrolepis exaltata (sword fern)

Arachniodes adiantiformis (leather fern)

Hosta leaves

Tellima grandiflora

Arum italicum 'Pictum'

The Drawing Room, Arbury Hall

THE DRAWING ROOM

This room has a barrel-vaulted ceiling. Inset in the panelling around the room are several full-length portraits.

A GLORIOUS VIEW

A large silver goblet is used to lift up this summer collection of perfumed freesia, sweet peas and carnations, evoking a warm summer's day. Shades of deep pink reflect the beautiful colours of exotic painted birds on the Chelsea dishes. Foliage has been used

A Glorious View (left)

FLOWERS

Gladiolus tubergenii 'Charm' (bridal gladiolus)

Chrysanthemum spray 'Snapper'

Freesia

Lathyrus odoratus (sweet pea)

Dianthus (perpetual-flowering pink carnation)

FOLIAGE

Chrysanthemum parthenium (matricaria)

Polygonatum (Solomon's seal)

Nephrolepis exaltata (sword fern)

sparingly, but where the bright green *Chrysanthemum parthenium* appears, it becomes very much a part of the design.

THE GALLERY

With its ribbed ceiling and arched bookcases in gothic style, the Gallery still retains some of its Elizabethan features.

MELODIOUS HARMONY

A room surrounded by dark panelling and multitudes of books requires soft, cheerful shades. The lemon and yellows of the freesias, lilies, 'Refour' chrysanthemum spray and cytisus (broom) lighten the room beautifully. The arrangement on the harpsichord spirals downwards, interlacing white antirrhinums, gladioli and cream stocks, chosen to reflect the ivory keys. The mechanics comprise a flat black tray easily concealed beneath the flowers and foliage, a brick of floral foam, with a third of a brick taped firmly on top for extra height. Using the natural line of the gladioli, repeating the curve at the top and the bottom, movement and balance are introduced to the completed piece.

FLOWERS

Antirrhinum majus (snapdragon)

Gladiolus 'White Friendship' (sword lily)

Matthiola incana (stocks/gilliflower)

Lilium 'Connecticut King' (lily)

Chrysanthemum (spider spray)

Freesia 'Fantasy'

Cytisus scoparius (broom)

FOLIAGE

Weigela

Laurus nobilis (bay)

Cornus alba 'Spaethii'

Hedera helix 'Glacier'

Melodious Harmony (opposite)

BLENHEIM PALACE

Driving north along the Stratford-upon-Avon road from Oxford, after some eight miles you will enter the old town of Woodstock, granted the Royal Charter in the fifteenth century. To the west of the town, encircled by a nine-mile dry stone wall, are the 2100 acres of parkland, landscaped by Capability Brown, in which stands the ancestoral home of the Dukes of Marlborough.

Blenheim Palace was built for John Churchill, 1st Duke of Marlborough, by Sir John Vanbrugh between the years 1705 and 1722, in recognition of his great victory at the battle of Blenheim 1704.

Blenheim Palace

Built on the grand scale, the palace and courts cover seven acres and the rooms range from the lofty pillared Great Hall, to gilded state rooms, to the spectacular Long Library.

The collection of fine furniture, paintings, sculpture and the world renowned set of tapestries *The Marlborough Victories* – depicting the Great Duke's famous battles – complement Vanbrugh's design. But Blenheim is still very much a home – warm, vibrant and full of life. There are no ghosts to chill the blood but there is the undeniable presence of its first owner and, perhaps its most famous son, Sir Winston Churchill.

THE PARKS AND GARDENS

The best approach to Blenheim is through Woodstock's narrow streets. The triumphal arch of the Woodstock gate leads to a view which Lord Randolph Churchill (father of Sir Winston) described as 'the finest view in England'. The towers of the Palace, Vanbrugh's Bridge, the poplared Elizabeth Island, the verdant slopes and the 135-foot high Column of Victory combine to create a panorama of glorious and dazzling beauty.

The Palace gardens, originally laid out by Henry Wise, Queen Anne's gardener, were altered along with the Park, by Brown, in the 1760s. The River Glyme was dammed to create the lake and the formal garden was replaced by sweeping lawns and a variety of rare and beautiful trees, cunningly planted to appear the work of nature rather than man. At the same time, the Great Court's cobble-stoned formality was replaced by a circle of grass. Slightly later the 5th Duke, recognized for his gardening skills by his work at Whiteknights (now Reading University) had the pleasure gardens with the lakeside paths, rock garden, grotto and pools built. In the early part of this century the 9th Duke and his architect, Achille Duchêne, restored formality to the east and west of the Palace with the delightful Italian Garden and the breathtaking Water Terraces. Today the 11th and present Duke is directing a 200-year plan to replace trees lost by age, disease (Dutch Elm disease destroyed, amongst the areas of woodland, the Grand Avenue in 1974) and the recent storm ravages. In this way, he intends to preserve the beauty of Blenheim's Park and Gardens, as envisaged by its eminent designers, for the enjoyment of future generations of visitors to come.

THE GREAT HALL

In such a vast, and in part severe, building, flowers are essential. The Great Hall is a very large room: its stone floor in white and black, stone walls, arched corridors and massive Corinthian pillars and central arch, all dominated by Thornhill's allegorical painting on the ceiling 67 feet above, state very clearly that no flower arrangement could be too large. But big arrangements need firm, sturdy containers; luckily a huge silver wine cistern (a reproduction of one of a set owned by the 1st Duke and taken on his campaigns) was available for use, and placed on a huge pink marble-topped table of the eighteenth century.

CHRISTMAS EXTRAVAGANZA

To catch the eye and to compete effectively in such bold surroundings tall and rich blooms were chosen, and fresh foliage was tipped with gold and silver for a seasonal splendour. A large trough-shaped container fitted snugly into the silver cistern and made a suitable waterproof liner. Two jumbo blocks (the largest foam available) were then securely taped in with waterproof sticky tape, and lowered in ready for use.

The Great Hall, Blenheim Palace
On the table, Christmas Extravaganza, and on
the pedestals, Seasonal Magic

The wax-like anthurium lilies act as the focal point, standing out from the varied selection of red blooms. Spiky gladioli form the height and width; gerberas, carnations, alstroemeria and lilies make up the centre of this design, completely obscuring the floral foam. The arrangement demonstrates how many shades of red can be used together successfully to form a perfect array of seasonal flowers. The whole display makes a brilliant impact on the cool and grandiose stone surrounds.

Christmas would not be Christmas without the presence of holly, ivy and spruce, which have been used in homes as seasonal decoration for centuries. Red-berried cotoneaster, adding a few winter fruits, trickles down with thin threads of periwinkle, ruscus and eucalyptus. The graceful lines spread onto the russet marble table and shimmer softly with the promise of Christmas.

Christmas Extravaganza

SEASONAL MAGIC

A pair of large round bowls have been used as bases this time for the stately 6-foot pedestal arrangements. As the completed designs were to be of such immensity, the stability of the base was of enormous importance. A jumbo block and two normal-sized bricks of floral foam were used on top and completely covered with $2\frac{1}{2}$ cm (1 in) wire netting, which was taped to the bowl to give additional support.

Flowers from far and wide have been gathered together for the two dramatic pedestal displays. Protea heads from Australia and South Africa, anthurium lilies from Holland, along with carnations from Columbia enhance this fiery selection. To add a festive sparkle and match the other arrangements, gilded hydrangea heads, ivy and spruce are used and glisten well against the dark green. The introduction of sprays of variegated holly enrich these stunning displays. Five golden glass baubles have been individually wired, then placed together at varying lengths and finally taped firmly to form a spray. The end wires act as a support when pushed into the floral foam. The completed setting in The Great Hall is set off by these opulent designs, which despite their size, remain graceful and serene, capturing that special *Seasonal Magic*.

FLOWERS AND FOLIAGE

Gladiolus (sword lily)

Gerbera 'Pascal' (Transvaal daisy)

Dianthus 'Scania' (perpetual-flowering carnation)

Dianthus 'Red Baron' (spray carnation)

Anthurium 'Favorite' (flamingo plant)

Lilium (lily)

Alstroemeria 'King Cardinal' (Peruvian lily)

Gilded and silvered *Hedera helix* (ivy)

Ilex aquifolum (variegated holly)

Danae racemosa (Alexandrian laurel or ruscus)

Cotoneaster horizontalis (cotoneaster)

Tsuga (western hemlock or sugar pine)

Arachniodes adiantiformis (leather fern)

Eucalyptus (gum tree)

FLOWERS AND FOLIAGE

Gladiolus (sword lily)

Gerbera 'Pascal' (Transvaal daisy)

Dianthus 'Scania' (perpetual-flowering carnation)

Dianthus 'Red Baron' (Spray carnation)

Anthurium 'Favorite' (flamingo plant)

Lilium (lily)

Alstroemeria 'King Cardinal' (Peruvian lily)

Protea (honeypot or sugarbush)

Hedera helix 'Goldheart' (ivy)

Vinca major 'Variegata' (periwinkle)

Gilded/silvered *Hedera helix* (ivy)

Ilex aquifolim (variegated holly)

Danae racemosa (Alexandrian laurel)

Cotoneaster horizontalis (cotoneaster)

Tsuga (western hemlock or sugar pine)

Arachniodes adiantiformis (leather fern)

Eucalyptus (gum tree)

Seasonal Magic (opposite)

CASTLE HOWARD

Castle Howard is one of the most spectacular stately homes in Britain, situated 15 miles north east of York, and surrounded by parklands and gardens. The design was conceived by John Vanbrugh in 1699, and executed in collaboration with Nicholas Hawksmoor – the team whose architectural expertise also contributed to Blenheim Palace. With Vanbrugh's creative imagination and Hawksmoor's practical ability, the home of the third Earl of Carlisle grew into a panoply of grandiose facades, walkways and courtyards, with a roof bedecked with statues and surmounted by a magnificent dome.

The House continued to adapt and develop long after Vanbrugh's demise. In 1940 a fire destroyed much of the South Front and all of the dome, but restoration work was undertaken and completed in 1960 under George Howard, the then owner. Today, the Hon. Mr and Mrs Simon Howard continue the bold and dedicated attention to detail in the restoration of Castle Howard, embodied not only in the grounds but also in the house.

FLOWERS AT CASTLE HOWARD
Mrs Simon Howard

There are some 20 rooms open to visitors, in the House, and during the season I ensure there are some 14 arrangements placed throughout these rooms. Often a successful display will disguise how much effort has gone into it in the preparation behind the scenes. The arrangements at Castle Howard are no exception. They have their birth, many months before I pick the flowers, in the garden. At every Chelsea Flower Show I make sure I am in the queue by 7.30 am so that I can get into the large flower hall as soon as it opens. Once inside, I note down names of plants and flowers which look especially attractive, and ideas come to me for arrangements in the House. Then a team of gardeners sets about a programme of planting for the year.

A week before the House opens I select the vases to be used for the whole season. This involves allocating one vase per room that will not change throughout the whole season. My little headquarters is the flower room. Here all vases, water buckets, floral foam, wire nests, secateurs, cloths and other such items are housed. It is not large, but it is mine!

The flowers are arranged and replaced twice a week, and despite the experience of five years, I always forget just how back-breaking the first morning is, what with all the bending involved in picking the flowers. Every Monday I set out at first light with all my dogs, and head for the gardens. Here I spend time picking and gathering all the flowers and loading them into the back of the car.

Back at the main House, I try to let the flowers have a chance to stand in water for a couple of hours, but this is not always possible: I like to have all the arrangements finished before the House opens at eleven o'clock. I try to make the arrangements informal. I want the visitors to feel that these flowers are arranged by the lady of the House for her friends, not something more in keeping with an exhibition or flower show. I think it is very important to make use of the colour schemes in the House, and I also concentrate on fragrance.

Lady Georgiana's Bedroom
Hybrid tea rose 'Sunblest'

In the Museum Room there is a beautiful old jardinière with a specially sealed bottom. I fill it with a huge vase, and sometimes go completely mad – once I put 50 gladioli in it. The jardinière lends itself to delphiniums and lilies as well, both of which I use regularly. I do enjoy these large arrangements, which enable me to fill out the flowers with foliage such as weigela, honeysuckle, elaeagnus or with cherry blossom. I also use fruits, and some times I try alliums, which, with their large heads, always create interest. The rooms in which the flowers are placed are left shut overnight,

The Museum Room
Lilium 'African Queen' (lily)

so when they are opened in the morning out wafts a rich mixture of aromas.

Once I have finished the arrangements, I clear out the flower room, which is always in a terrible mess – whoever said flower arranging was a tidy affair? Then I go round topping up the vases and making any little alterations I think necessary. Each Thursday evening I dismantle all the arrangements and prepare for a new set of displays for the following morning, when the whole process begins again.

The Arrangement on the Pedestal

LADY GEORGIANA'S BEDROOM
This arrangement has been placed in a silver rose bowl presented to the Hon. Mr and Mrs Simon Howard by the estate staff as a wedding present, and it sits on a Louis XV transitional bureau. Either side of it are two Crown Derby flower vases with landscapes painted on front and back.

MUSEUM ROOM
Here there is a Japanese vase filled with lilies, which is placed in the Jardinière. Behind and to the right of the arrangement are two landscapes of India painted by the 9th Earl of Carlisle. This room is devoted to his life and pictures.

THE ARRANGEMENT ON THE PEDESTAL
Climbing the Grand Staircase at the entrance of the House, the first arrangement one sees is this huge bowl of lilies (*Lilium* 'Regale') on a granite column. The powerful scent and the boldness of the arrangement is very much in keeping with the grandiose nature of the Entrance Hall.

GLAMIS CASTLE

G lamis Castle, near Dundee on the east coast of Scotland, is an impressive example of baroque architecture, with its array of wings, courtyards, and turrets of fine red granite. Home to Queen Elizabeth the Queen Mother, and birthplace of HRH Princess Margaret in 1930, this is a truly royal residence.

Glamis Castle. The Entrance Front in Spring

THE FLOWERS AND GARDENS

The parklands and gardens match the size and magnificence of the House itself. Landscaped in the style of Capability Brown, in the 1790s, they are sweeping and informal; a ha-ha separates the park from the lawns to provide an uninterrupted view. Other features have evolved more randomly, such as the Shrubbery laid out about 100 years ago, which gradually became overtaken by trees, originally planted to protect the shrubs. Now it is the impressive domain of larch, douglas fir, cypress, lime and beech, but it is still known as the Shrubbery even so. Similarly, a flower garden was planted 20 years ago with Christmas trees, which have grown higher than any house could accommodate!

Today, a proportion of the parkland is open to the public and a nature trail winds through the leafy Shrubbery. The gardens and the walkways are carefully maintained and continue to evolve, with a new herbaceous border in the Italian Garden and the Walled Garden once again yielding flowers and vegetables for the market place.

Flowers inside Glamis are very important, and the Queen Mother is renowned for her love of bright blooms. The Castle Administrator describes the historical and contemporary use of flowers at Glamis:

Flowers have always featured prominently in the Castle. In fact, a painting of the Great Drawing Room, dated 1931, showing HM Queen Elizabeth the Queen Mother's parents reading their golden wedding anniversary telegrams, features magnificent delphiniums. Today, a large vase of silk delphiniums is kept in the room, creating a sense of timelessness.

Arranging flowers in a castle the size of Glamis is not easy. A retired footman recently described how, in the 1930s, hyacinths were annually planted in bowls in each of the windows of the 142-step spiral staircase.

To meet the constant demand for floral arrangements, the gardens abound in flowers. In the spring, thousands of daffodils bloom in glorious abundance on both sides of the mile-long avenue. In the summer, there are magnificent mature azaleas and rhododendrons in the park and roses, including the 'Elizabeth of Glamis', which flower in the Dutch Garden. Nearby, is the Autumnal or Italian Garden, created by the Queen Mother's parents in 1910, and to supplement these sources of flowers is a five-acre Walled Garden. The latter with its extensive greenhouses, was designed in 1865 and noted between the Wars for the quality of its grapes.

THE GREAT DRAWING ROOM

This elegant, lofty, coral-coloured room, once the Great Hall, has a very Scottish and grand atmosphere. The walls are filled with family portraits, the largest and most notable being that of the 3rd Earl of Strathmore and Kinghorne and his sons, with their hunting dogs. Portraits of Lady Arbella Stuart, King Charles I and Queen Elizabeth I grace the wall beneath it.

The room is used regularly by the Strathmore family, and in the winter dried flowers provide a versatile yet decorative accompaniment to the regal surroundings.

The Great Drawing Room, Glamis Castle

FLOWERS AND FOLIAGE

Delphinium consolida (larkspur)

Centaurea macrocephala (yellow knapweed)

Ammobium

Eryngium planum (blue thistle)

Helichrysum (everlasting or strawflower)

Helichrysum thianshanicum (golden baby)

AUTUMN SHADES

Dried flowers can often look rather ineffective and harsh these days, especially when so many come in chichi baskets and dyed bunches are marketed widely. Here, colours have been chosen that are soft and muted, and the quantities are generous enough to make a dramatic impact amongst ornate surroundings.

The large arrangement on the piano, beside a photograph of Mary, Countess of Strathmore and Kinghorne, is made up of lepidium, hydrangeas, ammobiums, *Centaurea macrocephala*, eringiums and coral helichrysums. In the foreground of the room, a smaller display of heather with a tartan ribbon manages to be striking by being massed together without adornments.

THE LION IN WINTER

An arrangement of muted pinks, yellows and blues sits on a warm walnut table beside this tawny lion. Lions feature predominantly throughout the Castle and are contained in the Bowes Lyon coat of arms. The copper vase looks more appropriate than wicker here, and draws out the colours of the wood below. In fact the base of the arrangement is in a plain terracotta plant pot, which looks attractive in more modern surroundings.

Opium poppies stand out distinctly amongst the white and blue larkspur, hydrangeas, leek heads and lepidium. A vital splash of colour is then introduced with pink roses and red helichrysums. All three arrangements should last well through the winter, until the spring daffodils brighten the rooms of Glamis again.

FLOWERS AND FOLIAGE
Lepidium

Hydrangea

Helichrysum (everlasting or strawflower)

Helichrysum thianshanicum (golden baby)

Polygonum

Papaver somniferum (opium poppy)

Pink roses

Allium aflatunense (onion heads)

Delphinium consolida (blue larkspur)

Delphinium consolida (white larkspur)

HAGLEY HALL

Hagley Hall was the last of the great Palladian houses to be built in England. George, the 1st Lord Lyttelton, was mainly responsible for landscaping the grounds and for building this magnificent Palladian house between the years 1750 and 1760. Sanderson Miller drew up the final designs for Hagley Hall.

On Christmas Eve in 1925 much of Hagley was burnt down when a disastrous fire swept through the House, destroying the Library and many of the beautiful paintings. It was the 9th Viscount and his wife who lovingly restored the house to its former glory. The house is little changed to this day and still remains a much loved family home, occupied by the present Lyttletons, the Viscount and Viscountess Cobham. Flowers, for Lady Cobham are an essential element of life at Hagley:

Many years ago I was asked why we were redecorating a staircase. Words did not readily come to my lips, since I felt that the overshadowing gloom all around, caused by the pale mushroom paint, answered the question. My guest disagreed with me, by advising that country houses were meant to be gloomy. Since that day, most of the important rooms of our home have been redecorated, and whenever possible they are filled with flowers and plants to counter any suggestion of gloominess. Bright and vibrant flowers add the vital touch in bringing Hagley alive for visitors and family alike.

WHITE HALL

The entry to the house on the first floor, is filled with Italian features, commissioned by the 1st Lord Lyttelton, following his return from the Grand Tour. The Italian Francesco Vasali created the plasterwork for which the House is now famed, and on the far wall of the hall scagliola figures of Bacchus and Mercury are depicted as children in the roundels above. Recently, this room was renovated and the plasterwork, by then in heavy cobwebbed relief, was gently washed with soap and water, restoring it almost to its splendid condition of some 230 years before.

GRACEFUL CHARM

Painted in a delicate combination of white, lemon and yellow, the White Hall is a large room in which flowers can be displayed to their best advantage. However, it was still important to select an area of the Hall that would be best-enhanced and complemented by the arrangement and the end of the room, which was far enough away for the great archway not to dwarf the 7-foot arrangements, seemed most appropriate.

The two pedestals belonging to Lady Cobham were placed in either corner of the hall to soften the plasterwork, bringing an extra warmth and glow of sunshine to the cold stone scagliola figures. Large plastic bowls were used on the top of each pedestal, filled with green foam and covered with chicken wire to add extra support. The whole assembly was then secured to the container with green floral sticky tape.

The White Hall, Hagley Hall

Brilliant yellow is broken up with bold off-white, spiny-shaped chrysanthemum blooms, which form the focal point, following in a line through the centre of the display. Spider-spray chrysanthemums then link up and continue the theme with their similar petal formation, while gladioli add another paler shade establishing the outline. Lemon and gold daisy-like *Chrysanthemum* 'Delta' and dianthus form a union with the surrounding decor, broken by tiny, dainty droplets of gypsophila. This gleaming arrangement would be absolutely perfect for a special celebration as it takes full advantage of the attractive surroundings, leading you onwards, through the archway, to the rest of the house.

FLOWERS
Gladiolus (sword lily)
Dianthus (perpetual-flowering carnation)
Chrysanthemum (large blooms)
Chrysanthemum (spider spray)
Gypsophila paniculata (baby's breath)
Cream and yellow *Chrysanthemum* 'Delta'

FOLIAGE
Skimmia japonica

Graceful Charm (left)

FLOWERS
Gerbera (Transvaal daisy)
Dianthus ('Doris' pink)
Alstroemeria (Peruvian lily)
Astrantia major (masterwort)

FOLIAGE
Berberis thunbergii atropurpurea
Skimmia japonica
Arachniodes adiantiformis (leather fern)

CRIMSON DRAWING ROOM

The Drawing Room is a richly ornate room, dominated by a giltwood chandelier and a magnificent ceiling adorned with gold vines and cornucopias.

Even though the room has been decorated in deep crimson, it still appears very light. The sunlight streams in through a number of large windows along the left-hand side draped with curtains in a matching crimson fabric.

TIME STOOD STILL

Crimson velvety gerberas are the focal flowers in this front-facing display, lightened with pale Doris pinks and alstroemeria. The colours match the opulence of this room and link with crimson background of the table alcove. The clock above is a Louis XV boulle bracket timepiece by I. Langlois of Paris, given by Lord Spencer to his daughter when she married William Henry Lyttelton, who became Lord Lyttelton of the second creation. Beneath the flowers is a 1760 marble-topped side table.

Time Stood Still (opposite)

Chrysanthemum (single spray)

Gladiolus (sword lily)

Limonium sinuatum (statice or sea lavender)

Centaurea (knapweed)

Dianthus (spray carnation)

Dianthus (perpetual-flowering carnation)

Rosa 'Golden Times'

FOLIAGE

Arachniodes adiantiformis (leather fern)

Skimmia japonica

THE DINING ROOM

This is a very striking room with a rococo-style ceiling by Vassalli depicting winged putti flying amongst the clouds. A large oval dining table, with a rich mirror-glow, calls for a lavish and elongated arrangement, which can be viewed by all nineteen guests when seated around its circumference.

REFLECTIONS

A large, trough-shaped receptacle has been used for this display, filled with five bricks of water-retaining foam. The 2 in thick candle was positioned first, then pieces of foliage to build up the shape, then flowers in shades of white and yellow, with the fruit added last to avoid bruising. It is always interesting and fun to include fruit in an arrangement, and by the end of the dinner party it has often been eaten. Here however, the display is purely visual: the pineapple and coco heads have been sprayed with gold aerosol paint.

To anchor fruit well, cocktail sticks were used, or heavy skewers for heavier fruit. The wooden sticks – two or three depending on size – were pushed about half way into the base of the fruit, which was positioned in the arrangement with the sticks pushed into the floral foam.

As for the flowers, it was important to avoid a clash with the rich turquoise wall-covering; creams and yellows seemed a suitable option. The arrangement is low, as befits a dining table display, and the long-stemmed gladioli elongate the whole shape. On the polished wood, the flowers seem to float as if on a mill pond and their reflections travel deep into the dark wood grain.

THE GALLERY

The Gallery is a beautiful, long room stretching the length of the East Front, and displaying the family paintings. In the nineteenth century, the gallery was used for family cricket practices; this took its toll and the present generation has had the expense of repairing all the resultant damage. The decor is in shades of soft apricot and peach, with gold ceiling decoration and a beautiful, boldly carved chimney piece.

CAPTIVE BEAUTY

The mechanics for this circular display are a third of a brick of floral foam taped into a shallow container. As usual, the foliage is arranged first; flowers are added in stages using one variety at a time to build up to the completed piece. With this arrangement the Doris pinks were added first, and then alstroemeria and 'Gerdo' roses introduced. The two types of chrysanthemum sprays were then added to give depth, and soft misty pieces of gypsophila giving a light texture, were put in last.

The Gallery, Hagley Hall

FLOWERS
Dianthus ('Doris' pink)
Alstroemeria (Peruvian lily)
Pink *Chrysanthemum* 'Delta'
Gypsophila paniculata (baby's breath)
Chrysanthemum (spider spray)
Rosa 'Gerdo' (peach rose)

FOLIAGE
Fagus sylvatica 'purpurea' (copper beech)
Weigela 'Variegata'
Spiraea arguta
Skimmia japonica

HANCH HALL

This historic house was built in 1311 as the seat of the Aston family, and today is surrounded by small villages in the heart of Staffordshire. In the early days the estate itself stretched for many miles and included the village of Longdon.

There have been three main families connected with Hanch Hall: those at the time of Charles I were the Orme family, and then through marriage the estate passed to the Parkhurst and on to the Forster family. The present owners, Mr and Mrs Milton-Haynes, bought Hanch Hall in 1975, and moved to the hall during December of that year.

The house was in a terrible state of disrepair, with structural damage to most of the bedroom ceilings. Over the last few years the family has undertaken painstaking restoration work.

THE PARLOUR

This cosy little sitting room leads off the Georgian kitchen and is used regularly by the family. The solid oak fire surround is a magnificent feature in this room. Two Miserere panels, probably late fifteenth century, tell the story of Noah building the ark. Above them is a seventeenth-century carved frieze of cornucopia filled with fruit and acorns. Parchment deeds relating to Hanch Hall, one dated 1609, hang on the wall.

FIERY GLOW

Leaping tongues of red and gold flowers glow against the dark surround, their richness reflected in the brass beyond. In the depths of winter a glorious fire burns continuously and a similar fiery effect has been created, using golden eremurus, red gladioli, red spray and single-bloom carnations, deep orange lilies and

The Parlour, Hanch Hall (above)

FLOWERS AND FOLIAGE
Eremurus stenophyllus (foxtail lily)
Gladiolus (sword lily)
Chrysanthemum (spray)
Dianthus (spray carnation)
Cream and red *Dianthus* (carnation)
Rosa 'Gabrielle' (red rose)
Lilium (red lily)
Asparagus (fern)
Prunus laurocerasus (common laurel)

contrasting cream carnations. A black bowl ensured the container disappeared completely under the flowers and floral foam as the base allowed extra height and width. Minimal foliage allowed the black background to show through this warming display.

THE STAIRCASE

The staircase is an open-well design with a closed strapwork balustrade set in the Jacobean style. A panelled oak wall incorporating sixteenth and seventeenth-century frieze with gothic tracery lead up the stairs to a half-landing.

A GLORIOUS MORNING

This pedestal arrangement stands proudly at the foot of the staircase, bursting with life as the sun's rays softly touch each

The Staircase, Hanch Hall (right)

FLOWERS AND FOLIAGE

Carthamus tinctorius

Eremurus stenophyllus (foxtail lily)

Chrysanthemum 'Rivalry'

Dianthus (carnation)

Chrysanthemum (spider spray)

Prunus laurocerasus (common laurel)

Hosta (plantain lily)

Weigela variegata

Forsythia (golden bells)

57

flower. In this position, the arrangement can be seen from the back as well as the front, making it necessary for the design to be three-sided. The splendid, strong, sword-like eremurus gives a definite line to any arrangement and makes an attractive alternative to gladioli. *Carthamus tinctorius* has a fluffy, pompon flowerhead, rather like and orange thistle, giving the overall design a dramatic, spiky appearance. A smaller arrangement is situated at the top of the stairs, containing a similar selection of flowers to complete the total picture.

GEORGIAN BEDROOM

This room is dominated by the large, richly-draped, four-poster bed, reputedly slept in by Percy Bysshe Shelley. The green and pink furnishings and embroidered Victorian table top set the tone for an airy and romantic display.

PINK POETRY

The hand-painted jug stands on a matching glass tray, making a charming companion to this dainty bouquet set in a wickerwork container. A summer selection reflects the full colour co-ordination of the surroundings with larkspur, brodiaea and spray chrysanthemums.

Wonderfully scented *Dianthus* 'Doris', known as a modern pink, came into being by crossing an old-fashioned pink with a perpetual flowering carnation; the hybrid *D. allwoodii* was produced, which later became the parent of modern pinks. Their delicate perfume could not be confused with any other flower, giving both colour and beauty.

THE MORNING ROOM

Mrs Milton-Haynes, the present owner of Hanch hall, describes the effect of flowers in this eighteenth-century room.

This morning room had stood abandoned and neglected for many years. When we bought the house in 1975 we were determined that eventually every one of the 32 rooms should take on its own character again. The large window overlooks the sandstone arches of the porte-cochère (the gateway for vehicles leading to the courtyard), but the greatest delight is when the sun floods in on a summer's morning. It dazzles you. In the bay with

FLOWERS

Chrysanthemum 'Remember'

Delphinium consolida (Larkspur)

Brodiaea

Erica (heather)

FOLIAGE

Artemisia ludoviciana

Cineraria maritima

Pink Poetry (opposite)

*original hand-made window panels still intact, there is a mahogany
breakfast table which belonged to my grandfather. Here is where I write to
friends and where my children have written many thank you letters. If you
look carefully there is my grandfather's name scribbled some three-
quarters of a century ago, a young boy's signature inscribed forever on the
surface.*

*Cream and ivory are favourite colours here. The flowers I choose for this
room are white and yellow, with a touch of orange sometimes. I love them
in abundance on the mahogany table; they range from white narcissi in the
spring to asters and chrysanthemums in winter.*

*I consider no room to be complete without a coup de grâce of floral
arrangements appropriate to it, so all through the year from spring to
autumn I keep fresh arrangements, varying in size and character from a
tiny posy, to one or two choice blooms balancing precariously in a tear
glass, to a great symphony of colour.*

*White figures on the table are Parian ware, and hugging the table are
four Edwardian chairs upholstered in cream. There are some nineteenth-
century stumpwork pictures on the wall, oil paintings and a collection of
oriental lacquered pictures of orchids and carnations. The morning room is
quiet and serene; the eighteenth-century elegance has indeed returned.*

CREAM ELEGANCE

Cream is soft and subtle, but by introducing yellow or orange the mood can change from a restful piece to something more alert and joyous. Just a simple touch of a vibrant colour add that extra warmth and rich quality that this room deserves.

The poppy-heads have been bleached and the seedheads cut in half to expose the intricate structure inside. The spider-spray chrysanthemums then add drama with their irregular petal formation. Dainty sprays of cream Singapore orchids, with their heavenly little flowers, are then introduced to create an overall harmony here.

FLOWERS

Chrysanthemum (spider spray)
Chrysanthemum 'White Delta'
Dendrobium (Singapore orchid)
Dianthus (carnation)

FOLIAGE

Vinca (periwinkle)
Forsythia (golden bells)

The Colour of England

FLOWERS AND FOLIAGE
Philadelphus (mock orange)
Centaurea (knapweed or corn flower)
Dianthus (carnation)
Brodiaea
Gypsophila paniculata (baby's breath)
Sorbaria arborea (spiraea)

THE OAK ROOM
Mrs Milton-Haynes
Another room rescued. What I particularly like about the oak room is that it has not been painted since the nineteenth century. Admittedly, we have graduated from candles to electricity. Apart from that, I have rejected any cosmetic changes to this room. I have tried to recreate my grandfather's oak panelled library as I remember it as a child – a happy and inviting room, dominated by the large oak refectory table and

The Oak Room, Hanch Hall

handsome Charles II red velvet chairs. With its dark-beamed ceiling, it is vital to lighten the room, and this is usually achieved by introducing brightly coloured flowers that 'lift' the beams.

The shades of the red, white and blue Minton plates which now hang around the walls are here picked up by the flowers, which echo the colour on the table and oak bureau. The window opens out onto a lawn and seventeenth-century garden filled with Elizabethan summer flowers, grown specially for the house; perfume from the honeysuckle, roses and lavender drifts indoors on a warm day.

THE COLOUR OF ENGLAND

Dark, English oak panelling makes a formal backdrop for this patriotic display, inspired by the Minton plates on the wall. The richly coloured flowers are striking but not overbearing, as the introduction of blue corn flowers and white orange blossom, picked from the garden, softens the vibrant colours and breaks the regimented effect of the carnations.

63

HOLME PIERREPONT HALL

Holme Pierrepont Hall is surrounded by peaceful countryside in Nottinghamshire, although only 4 miles from Nottingham town centre. The house, built by Sir William Pierrepont in the early days of Henry VIII's reign, is a redbrick manor house, now home to Mr and Mrs Robin Brackenbury. The Pierrepont line comes through Mrs Brackenbury's side of the family, and with her husband she enjoys restoring the courtyard gardens of this ancient house and providing fresh flowers for the interiors.

Mrs Brackenbury

Our courtyard garden was laid out in 1875 and has an elaborate boxhedge parterre filled with various herbs, hosta and grey-leafed plants. In the spring we grow tulips and wallflowers there. My style of flower arranging is simply to go into the garden and pick whatever is in flower – without robbing it completely, of course. I tend really just to plonk flowers in a vase, and in some cases don't even use foliage – especially with daffodils and polyanthus – because I think it sometimes looks better that way. At other times, I do a whole arrangement without flowers: the dark red leaves of copper beech in the spring look wonderful in a vase.

The flowers I value most are those that get us through the winter: flowering azaleas and hyacinths, for instance. Then the long, dark winter days make spring all the more exciting and I wait with baited breath for the first camellias to flower and dart out each day to look at my Paeonia lutea *(tree peony), which has simply wonderful rich flowers in May.*

FLOWERS
Alstroemeria 'Zebra' (Peruvian lily)
Chrysanthemum (yellow bloom)
Chrysanthemum (single spray)

FOLIAGE
Nephrolepis exaltata
Ananas comusus (pineapple plant)
Sedum
Pyracantha
Actinidia kolomikta
Hedera algeriensis

LOWER LODGINGS

You enter a bygone age when you step onto the stone floor of this heavily beamed room. Most of the furniture is from the seventeenth and nineteenth century, including a pair of oval brass-edged tables from *HMS Nile*, Admiral Nelson's flagship.

POT-ET-FLEUR

For a pot-et-fleur arrangement, a large round or oval bowl is best, with either the plants planted directly into the potting soil or the pots nestled into a layer of soil with a little gravel underneath for drainage, which is better as it allows each plant to be given its own individual watering requirements. For the flowers, a round dish is needed, or even a plastic container fitted with a good size piece of foam, placed firmly in the space between the plants.

The way the planted foliage flows indicates the shape and line which should be followed through with the flowers. Here, Nephrolepis fern has been chosen, which flows freely; the variegated pineapple plant, with its strong and definite shape; and *Hedera canariensis*, for its trailing qualities. Large golden chrysanthemums, alstroemeria and single spray chrysanthemums intertwine between the plant material to create this unusually striking display. Small pieces of additional foliage and moss may be needed to fill gaps and to camouflage the mechanics.

Pot-et-fleur

An arrangement like this is enjoyable to put together and makes a pleasant change from flowers on their own. It will, of course, last some considerable time if you replace the odd flower as it fades.

THE MASTER BEDROOM

Superbly timbered, this room dates back to the early 1500s and is softly decorated in shades of apricot and peach.

COUNTRY BASKET

'Delight' roses, alstroemeria and honeysuckle have been placed together in this simple country basket. A small plastic saucer holds the floral foam in place, acting as a waterproof lining. Tiny

FLOWERS

Rosa 'Darling' (rose)

Gypsophila paniculata (baby's breath)

Alstroemeria 'Rosita'

Chrysanthemum (single spray)

Lonicera (honeysuckle)

Fagus sylvatica 'purpurea' (copper beech)

Berberis thunbergii atropurpurea

Cineraria maritima

Stachys lanata (lambs' ears)

Country Basket (left)

blossoms of single chrysanthemum sprays are deeply recessed; the open roses then become a feature. Curved pieces of soft grey velvety stachys and *cineraria maritima* fall naturally onto the oval table. Honeysuckle and wine-coloured berberis continue the outline, giving the design an informal look. Specks of gypsophila 'Bristol Fairy' appear like a web draped through the flowers.

VICTORIAN BEDROOM

This grand four-poster bed was made in Nottinghamshire in 1860 and the hangings and bedcover are reproductions of Victorian chintz in restful shades of cream and green.

GUEST'S WELCOME

In this arrangement, detail had to be added to the back of the design, enabling it to be viewed from behind. Delicate green, cream and white fabrics and pale lilac walls have been followed through into the flowers. At the highest point, lilac-scented stocks appear, sweeping gracefully through the design. Sprigs of alstroemeria trickle down the centre and paler shades are placed in the outline. Delicate sprays of astrantia picked from the garden give a sense of movement. The budded hosta flowerheads add a softer green and another texture with their prickly appearance. Carnations and Doris pinks continue to be inserted throughout, introducing further shades of pink, and creating a warm welcome for any visitor.

FLOWERS

Alstroemeria (Peruvian lily)

Astrantia major (masterwort)

Dianthus ('Doris' pink)

Dianthus (pink carnation)

Matthiola (stock)

Hosta (flower)

FOLIAGE

Hosta (foliage)

Echinops (globe thistle)

Mentha citrata bergamot (mint)

Guest's welcome (opposite)

FLOWERS
Chrysanthemum (white single spray)
Gypsophila paniculata (baby's breath)

FOLIAGE
Sorbaria arborea
Hosta aureo-marginata

THE BLUE BEDROOM

A beautifully hand-carved rosewood bed, which was made in India, is the main feature of the Blue Bedroom. The fashionable blue and white curtains and matching bed hangings are originals designed by William Morris. On the wall is a fine oil painting of Mrs Paul Sprigman and her daughter Mrs R. H. L. Brackenbury by Richard Jack painted around 1912.

BLUE MOOD

Crisp, white posies resembling white caps or frothy surf against the deepest aquamarine ocean create the *Blue Mood*. A pair of simple and dainty all-round arrangements stand out well against the blue wall-covering and the dark rosewood, brass-inlaid card tables at either side of the bed on which they are displayed. These circular posies were designed in round plastic dishes containing one third of a brick of floral foam. With single white chrysanthemum spray and gypsophila, they would grace any home.

KEDLESTON HALL

he building of this grand house was started in 1759 for Sir Nathaniel Curzon, the 1st Baron Scarsdale. Having just returned from a tour of Italy with new ideas, the young Scotsman Robert Adam designed Kedleston Hall in classical style, with huge, splendid columns and pillars of marble. The alabaster used was excavated from the family's own quarries at Ratcliffe-on-Soar.

Kedleston Hall was taken over by The National Trust in March 1987 but is still the home of the Curzon family. Flowers can be found in most of the rooms at Kedleston today and are arranged by volunteers.

Victorian Elegance

FLOWERS AND FOLIAGE

Chrysanthemum (shaggy daisy)

Gladiolus 'White Friendship' (sword lily)

Hydrangea

Dryopteris (fern)

Sambucus racemosa 'Plumosa aurea' (golden elder)

Sorbaria arborea

Prunus laurocerasus (common laurel)

Hedera helix (ivy)

THE MUSIC ROOM

Decorated in a rich coral shade, this room houses an array of beautiful instruments, including a large gilded organ cased in mahogany by Adam. Landscapes, flower paintings and portraits fill the walls and provide a homely feeling. Here there are two very different arrangements on view in the same room.

VICTORIAN ELEGANCE

Standing on a harpsichord, made in 1760 by Kirkwood, is an unusually-shaped arrangement, brimming over with white gladioli, hydrangea and shaggy daisy. Flowers and foliage are displayed together, following through with numerous shades of green. Textures of shining formal shapes, spiky and dull green intermingle to give a superb informal design, overlooked by the photograph of Queen Victoria. The display raised upon a wooden plinth allows the ivy to tumble downwards and lengthen the whole arrangement.

ENGLISH COUNTRY GARDEN

For this arrangement Lady Scarsdale's fine, brightly coloured container, with small golden goat-like hooves, is filled with a selection of large, rust-coloured chrysanthemums mixed with alstroemeria, spray carnations, gerberas and chincherinchees, reflecting beautifully the colours in the container. The bronze Mayford blooms with their rich hue, link the arrangement to the table and the wall colouring to the arrangement. Extended curves of forsythia foliage spill over the edge, and the fluffy flowerheads of the sorbaria, toning with the gerbera, soften the design.

FLOWERS

Dianthus (spray carnation)

Alstroemeria (Peruvian lily)

Gerbera (Transvaal daisy)

Chrysanthemum 'Bronze Mayford' (blooms)

Orithogalum thyrsoides (chincherinchee)

FOLIAGE

Forsythia (golden bells)

Sorbaria arborea

English Country Garden

Happy Days

FLOWERS AND FOLIAGE
Rosa 'Golden Times' and 'Coed' (rose)
Freesia 'Fantasy'
Erica (heather)
Hedera helix 'Goldheart'
Vinca major (periwinkle)
Euonymus

FLOWERS AND FOLIAGE
Hydrangea macrophylla
Phlox paniculata
Lavandula spica (lavender)
Clematis 'Jackmanii Superba'
Eryngium variifolium (sea holly)
Echinops banaticus (globe thistle)
Mentha rotundifolia (apple mint – in flower)
Rosa 'Gerdo' (peach rose)
Hosta (flowers)
Sorbaria arborea
Mahonia japonica (berries)
Bergenia cordifolia (elephant's ear)

Roses of Summer (opposite)

THE STATE DRAWING ROOM

The State Drawing Room has a very different feel to the Music Room, although alabaster appears again here around the doorways and windows. The ceiling is full of colourfully detailed plasterwork, with a Waterford crystal chandelier, which makes a beautiful centre-piece. Several fine pieces of Blue John, or Derbyshire Spar, are displayed in this room.

ROSES OF SUMMER

Complementing the hues of these blue damask wall hangings is this lovely summer design. A blue haze of *Clematis jackmanii*, hydrangea, eryngium, globe thistle and phlox, intertwined with peachy-pink rose 'Gerdo', captures the mood of a summer's day. The rich purple-blue clematis spills out over the rim of the blue bowl. Spiny thistle heads add another textured shape, with pieces of phlox giving the outline.

Soft peach roses dotted amongst the other flowers lift the design. Large, shiny veined bergenia leaves fan out from the centre to reveal recessed lavender and the blackcurrant-coloured mahonia berries.

THE LIBRARY

In a completely different style, this room contains a superbly decorated ceiling in the original shades of soft blues and pinks. The wall colouring is a soft green with marble appearing in the fireplace, and the bookcases, designed by Robert Adam, make a lovely backcloth for the arrangements.

HAPPY DAYS

'Golden times' and 'Coed' roses and cream freesia gleam together with 'Golden Heart' ivy and periwinkle with just a touch of white heather, overflowing onto the dark wood desk.

Arrangements do not always have to follow tradition or be symmetrically balanced; this one-sided cascade does not smother the desk but leaves the drawers visible as it spills over the edge. For a writing desk such as this, a neat and discreet arrangement is practical and attractive, and allows the ornaments and photographs to be viewed simultaneously.

GARDEN SURPRISE

Here is an arrangement with a difference, as it combines fresh and dried materials. A selection of dried material of different shapes and sizes forms a striking floral array, with brown bullrushes giving height to the design, and grasses and coco heads mounted on stems adding interest. The whole design is carried out in exactly the same way as a fresh floral display. Dried material is integrated so it becomes a part of the design and does not appear to be an afterthought. As fresh flowers have been used with dried material, the base used is the normal water-retaining floral foam (usually green). If dried grasses alone were being used in arrangement, dry floral foam (usually brown) would be best.

FLOWERS

Ornithogalum thyrsoides (chincherinchee)

Chrysanthemum 'Refour' and spider spray

Rosa 'Golden Times' (yellow rose)

Lilium 'Connecticut King' (lily)

Dianthus (spray carnation)

FOLIAGE

Ligustrum ovalifolium 'Aureum'

Hedera helix 'Goldheart' (ivy)

Hosta

Dried grasses, *scirpus* (bulrush), coco heads

Hedera helix (ivy)

Vinca major (periwinkle)

THE STATE BOUDOIR

When planning this large room, Robert Adam created an unusual effect by dividing it with a screen of columns. Contained within this soft turquoise-blue interior are several family paintings, peering out from the 'royal-icing' columns.

THROUGH THE LOOKING GLASS

Blue can be such a cold colour, but here the introduction of heavy apricot, gold curtains adds a warm glow at the windows.

Apricot and peachy-pink shades are chosen for the arrangement shown overleaf to follow through to the ornately decorated gilt looking-glass. Dark green foliage throws the display away from the background and gives a strong but definite shape. For the mechanics, a large round bowl and three full bricks of floral foam are used, cut to fit the container, then covered with chicken wire, taped in firmly.

Curved lines of the dark weigela form part of the height, then large chrysanthemums are introduced in tiers, followed through

The State Boudoir, Kedleston Hall
Through the Looking Glass (and see overleaf)

FLOWERS AND FOLIAGE
Fuchsia magellanica 'Gracilis'

Alstroemeria (Peruvian lily)

Chrysanthemum 'Peach Cassandra' (bloom and spray)

Gypsophila paniculata (baby's breath)

Dianthus (spray carnation)

Dianthus (perpetual-flowering carnation)

Salix matsudana 'Tortuosa'

Cineraria maritima

Parthenocissus (Virginia creeper)

Veronica incana

Artemisia ludoviciana

Weigela

with carnations and alstroemeria. Gentle pieces of weeping fuschia give extra detail, so too does the virginia creeper trailing at the bottom. Small sprays of gypsophila and grey pieces of senecio are tucked in behind the blooms to relieve the dark green a little.

SMALL DELIGHT

Through the columns is an additional, small oval-ended room (above). A softer colour selection than that used in the main part of the room is needed, as the surrounding furnishings are quite dark. Using pale cream gerberas with their dark centres, the rich deep tones of the wooden door panelling and circular table top are suggested. Not all arrangements in great rooms have to be large and grand; here, this round ceramic bowl demonstrates the satisfaction of small but beautiful.

FLOWERS
Gerbera (Transvaal daisy)

Alstroemeria (Peruvian lily)

Dianthus (spray carnation)

Cream *Dianthus* (perpetual-flowering carnation)

Gypsophila paniculata (baby's breath)

Chrysanthemum (single spray)

FOLIAGE
Leycesteria firmosa (pheasant berry)

Eucalyptus (gum tree)

Senecio maritima 'Silver Dust'

Salix matsudana 'Tortuosa'

Spiraea arguta

RAGLEY HALL

Ragley Hall, the home of the Marquess and Marchioness of Hertford, is situated in the heart of Warwickshire countryside. The original architect was Robert Hooke, and after the planning was complete, the Earl of Conway began building Ragley in 1680. Today, the home is open to the public, and flowers are an intrinsic but time-consuming part of its welcome, as Lord Hertford knows only too well!

He describes the importance of flowers at Ragley:

I always think a room without flowers looks unfinished, like an unframed picture or an empty fireplace. If it is in a stately home which people actually pay to see, then at least one vase, and preferably two or three, is vital.

When my wife and I first opened Ragley to visitors, the house had been empty for some years and had a thoroughly stale and depressing atmosphere: a cold fug mixed with the smells of dry rot and pesticide. Log fires helped; but flowers made all the difference.

Scent, to me, is far more important than appearance. Daffodils may look like spring; narcissi smell of it. The only perfect flower is the rose: its smell matches its beauty. So when my wife complained one summer's morning that the task of filling every room with roses was exhausting, I gladly volunteered to do it. Having filled a basket with the very best roses in the garden, I arranged a stunningly beautiful vase in the green drawing room. It took time, but the result was immensely satisfying. As I was admiring my handiwork, my wife came in and agreed that I had done well. Then she asked, 'What about the other rooms? We open in half an hour.' I had spent the whole morning on one vase. So now we have a professional who fills the house with scent and beauty in no time at all.

THE STUDY

The study is a warm and friendly room decorated in rich coral and gold. The portrait of the 1st Marquess, hanging above the fireplace, was painted by George Morland.

CORAL CASCADE

The flowers in this room blend softly with their surroundings. By introducing cream hyacinths, which delicately perfume the room, a colour link is made with the fire surround. Additional coral-coloured gladioli, carnations and chrysanthemums reflect the rich wall-covering, creating a perfect colour combination.

Because the study is such a strong coral, this two-coloured arrangement has to remain as simple as possible, with an uncomplicated style. A natural design has been created by encouraging the flowers to cascade softly onto the tabletop. As the container forms no visual part of this display, a simple dish is quite suitable. The flowers and plant material must completely cover the mechanics. Waterproof sticky tape secures the floral foam to the dish.

FLOWERS
Gladiolus (sword lily)
Chrysanthemum (apricot single spray)
Hyacinthus (cream hyacinth)
Chrysanthemum 'Refour'
Dianthus (spray carnation)

FOLIAGE
Melaleuca
Viburnum tinus
Euonymus
Eucalyptus (gum tree)

THE RED SALOON

This lush, red room remains exactly as it was when designed in 1780 by Wyatt. It is quite remarkable that on the two occasions when the Louis XVI furniture was re-covered, the pattern and colour of the original was found and the material matched perfectly. The room boasts a wealth of colourful and interesting paintings dating back from the early seventeenth century.

A TOUCH OF GOLD

In this arrangement gilded rhododendron and ivy leaves with rich carnations create an opulence of golds and deep reds, lifted slightly by the soft cream lily and spider-spray chrysanthemums. The design has been tailored especially for this table; it does not overpower the delicate items displayed around it and yet it is large enough to be viewed from all angles in the room.

Coral Cascade in the Study (above), and the Red Saloon (right), Ragley Hall

FLOWERS

Gladiolus (sword lily)

Chrysanthemum (red single spray)

Chrysanthemum 'Refour' (gold)

Chrysanthemum (cream spider spray)

Dianthus (red spray carnation)

Dianthus (perpetual-flowering red carnation)

Lilium 'Sterling Star' (lily)

Lilium 'Red Night' (lily)

Freesia

FOLIAGE

Rhododendron (sprayed with gold spray paint)

Hedera helix (ivy sprayed gold)

Buxus sempervirens (box)

Eucalyptus (gum tree)

A Touch of Gold

For the mechanics green foam is secured firmly with floral sticky tape; a simple pedestal-style vase is used to raise the whole arrangement from the table and place the emphasis on the flowers.

The gold foliage subtly reflects gilt in the furniture and picture frames. Simply use a good quality gold spray paint; only use foliage that is totally dry before spraying begins and, of course, all spraying should always be done out of doors on a covered surface. The finished product must be left to dry for several hours and can then be used in the normal way amongst flowers and will remain fresh for some considerable time.

FLOWERS

Cymbidium (orchid)

Chrysanthemum (spider spray)

Gerbera (Transvaal daisy)

Tulipa (tulip)

Freesia (white)

Dianthus (orange spray carnation)

Dianthus (perpetual-flowering carnation)

Lilium 'Prominence' (lily)

Mahonia 'Charity' and *M. aquifolium*

Cytisus (broom)

Buxus sempervirens (box)

THE GREEN DRAWING ROOM

The flowers are displayed on a grand eighteenth-century French commode, made by Schmidt, with a black and gold candelabra on either side, made by Matthew Boulton (1728-1809). The Chinese gold Chippendale mirror and pieces of delicate Meissen china complete this beautiful setting.

GOLDEN GLORY

A combination of apricot gerberas link beautifully with the colour of the French commode and are accompanied by single chrysanthemum sprays and deeper orange lilies. The spider blooms break up the formation, introducing some of the paler wall colouring into the design. A gorgeous stem of orchids rises up proudly out of the centre. Freesia, hyacinths and mahonia fall out near the base, all

competing with their strong fragrances. Their creamy colouring complements the Meissen china surrounding them, and finally a few tulips are positioned, just to indicate the arrival of spring. The completed piece is displayed in a pedestal-style container belonging to Lady Hertford, used regularly for flowers at Ragley Hall.

THE MAUVE DRAWING ROOM
A QUIET MOMENT

The arrangement here in the Mauve Drawing Room would complement any home as the flowers are simple and the size is convenient for most tables. Chrysanthemum spray 'Penny Lane' picks up shades of the soft mauve of the wall, and colours of the surrounding furnishings are found again amongst the flowers. This tiny display with its dainty formation of freesia and daisy-like chrysanthemums is made all the more pretty by the viburnum buds and gypsophila.

FLOWERS
Chrysanthemum 'Beppie' (single spray)
Dianthus (pink carnation)
Freesia (pink and lilac)
Gypsophila paniculata (baby's breath)
Helleborus orientalis (hellebore)
Hyacinthus (blue hyacinth)

FOLIAGE
Viburnum tinus
Eucalyptus (gum tree)
Berberis darwinii
Lonicera nitida

FLOWERS
Chrysanthemum 'Penny Lane'
Freesia (pink and lilac)
Gypsophila paniculata (baby's breath)

FOLIAGE
Viburnum tinus
Berberis darwinii
Eucalyptus (gum tree)
Lonicera nitida

FLORAL INTERLUDE
This Viennese piano, made by Bosendorfer in 1860, makes an ideal base for this arrangement of freesias, chrysanthemum spray 'Beppie' and carnations. The mother-of-pearl and tortoise-shell piano keys softly echo their colours and link beautifully with the arrangement above.

THE PRINCE REGENT'S BEDROOM

The grandeur of the name is matched by the decor. Richly decorated in coral, peach, gold, creamy white, there is a strong influence of black adding a masculine air to the room. The bed was specially built for the Prince of Wales when he visited Ragley in 1796, and has seventeenth-century, hand-painted silk curtains. It was here in this very room that the Prince was awoken with the tragic news of the death of his only child, Princess Charlotte. The large painting over the fireplace is a portrait of the Prince Regent by Lawrence, and the black sofa is a Victorian *tête-à-tête* with a table in the centre.

A SIMPLE BEDSIDE ARRANGEMENT

This is a dreamy bedside arrangement of cream lilies, spider chrysanthemum spray with just a touch of orange spray carnation reflecting the shades of rust in the silk curtains. The arrangement is quite simple in style and yet not out of place in these regal surroundings.

FLOWERS
Chrysanthemum (spider spray)
Lilium 'Siver Star' (lily)
Dianthus (spray carnation)
Forsythia (golden bells)

FOLIAGE
Skimmia japonica
Cupressus (cypress)

The Library, Ragley Hall

THE LIBRARY

The Library at Ragley is used by Lord and Lady Hertford as their main living room. From the window there is a glorious view over the lake to the Cotswold hills beyond.

EASTER MORNING

There is spring in the air this Easter morning, and it is especially important to create a vivid and fresh arrangement. Some 10,000 books of varying shapes, sizes and colour tones, make a splendid back-cloth for the two bright, glowing floral displays. With the shafts of golden sunlight gently touching the petals of the daffodils, forsythia and catkins the whole scene bursts into life and suggests the vigour of spring.

Easter morning

FLOWERS

Narcissus (double cream)

Chrysanthemum (double yellow)

Chyrsanthemum (bronze single and spider spray)

Chrysanthemum (yellow and bronze spider spray)

Dianthus (spray carnation)

FOLIAGE

Salix caprea (pussy willow)

Mahonia aquifolium

Elaeagnus pungens 'Maculata'

Laurus nobilis (bay)

Forsythia (golden bells)

It is often difficult to get daffodils to go into the floral foam but there is an easy way around that: use a pencil to make the hole first and then by guiding the stem into that hole, the daffodil can be firmly inserted into the water-retaining base.

THE SOUTH STAIRCASE HALL

This mural is a truly magnificent work of art and was completed in 1983 by Graham Rust. It is painted in indelible gouache on a heavy pure rag paper. All the ceiling work is painted directly onto the plaster and depicts the Mount of Temptation, and lower down Lord and Lady Hertford's four children, along with their godparents, are pictured on the balcony. Behind the floral pieces, the two mirrors, which have been incorporated in the design, are by Chippendale, and the surrounding mural, full of brightly coloured butterflies, birds, monkeys and other animals, took nearly 14 years to complete.

REGAL SPLENDOUR

Although at a glance this area may seem full of different colour schemes, when it actually comes to choosing shades and planning the arrangements, reds and coral pinks seem the perfect choice. Small sections of red and orange appear on nearly every wall. Cream longiflorum lilies are chosen with gladioli, tulips and a stem of cymbidium orchid rising up from the centre; carnations are interspersed throughout the arrangement and gerberas add solidity to the shape.

FLOWERS
Tulipa (tulip)

Lilium longiflorum (lily)

Dianthus (perpetual-flowering carnation)

Cymbidium (orchid)

Gerbera (Transvaal daisy)

Gladiolus (sword lily)

Gypsophila paniculata (baby's breath)

FOLIAGE
Eucalyptus (gum tree)

Buxus sempervirens (box)

Lonicera nitida (honeysuckle)

ROCKINGHAM CASTLE

*D*riving along through the park to the entrance and past the Great Gatehouse at Rockingham, one is overwhelmed by the feeling of travelling back in time and by a powerful sense of history. The Castle stands as a prominent landmark in the Welland Valley in Leicestershire and was built by William the Conqueror as a fortress for guarding against intrusion from the north. Many kings have lived or stayed here, including Henry III, Edward I, and Henry V, who was the last king in residence.

In 1544 Edward Watson obtained Rockingham from Henry VIII and converted it from a mediaeval castle into a domestic residence. During the Civil War, however, the Castle was taken from the Watsons by Lord Grey, fighting for Cromwell; he kept it from the Royalists until the end of the war, when it was returned to Sir Lewis Watson badly damaged. Ever since then, restored and repaired, it has been in the hands of the Watsons. Today, Mr and Mrs Michael Saunders Watson live there, and Mrs Saunders Watson helps in maintaining the garden and preparing flowers:

I love gardening and have had enormous pleasure planting two herbaceous borders in the Rose Garden. I also try to use flowers and shrubs that are growing in the garden to decorate the house. When the cherry blossom is out, the rooms are filled with its large sprays, and the same goes for delphiniums. Usually, we tend to choose plants for the house that like cool conditions, and we have a great deal of fun picking them from garden catalogues. However, I must admit that even these plants prefer the greenhouse, as Rockingham lacks light and humidity. Yet the plants do cheer up a dark corner and fill the room with a sense and scent of well-being and love.

THE LONG GALLERY

This very long room with its rich reds and golds was the main Drawing Room of the Castle in 1883. The long gallery houses many beautiful paintings, including works by Sir Peter Lely, Sir Joshua Reynolds and Ben Marshall. The set of fine walnut chairs with carved backs in the style of Queen Anne are early Victorian.

MID-SUMMER SPLENDOUR

This beautifully carved wooden pedestal, belonging to Mrs Saunders Watson, is an ideal base on which to display such an abundance of richly coloured flowers. Three large bricks of floral foam have been used, inside a deep round bowl. Such a large display requires a very firm base securely taped in. The grey foliage of eucalyptus, which complements the rich reds and pinks so well, is used with dainty sweet peas to give the room an overwhelming scent. The sweet peas appear to burst out from the middle down either side, adding a softer delicate look to this large design.

Cerise pink gerberas with their black eyes draw attention to the dark pedestal, repeating the colour of the chairs and dado panelling. This display reaches its peak with red gladioli and

FLOWERS
Lathyrus odoratus (sweet pea)

Alstroemeria 'King Cardinal' (Peruvian lily)

Pink *gerbera* (Transvaal Daisy)

Pink *Dianthus* (perpetual-flowering carnation)

Dianthus (spray carnation)

Gladiolus (sword lily)

Chrysanthemum 'Lilac Byoux'

FOLIAGE
Berberis thunbergii atropurpurea

Tsuga (western hemlock or sugar pine)

Hedera helix (ivy)

Eucalyptus (gum tree)

Cotoneaster salicifolius

Viburnum tinus

The Long Gallery

FLOWERS

Chrysanthemum 'Penny Lane'

Freesia 'Jessica' (pink freesia)

Lathyrus odoratus (sweet pea)

Dianthus (spray carnation)

FOLIAGE

Prunus laurocerasus

Viburnum tinus

Hebe (veronica)

Eucalyptus (gum tree)

Pittosporum tenuifolium

alstroemeria falling away softly in a natural curve. Red follows a line through the centre, the spray carnations taking you back towards the outline.

The Broadwood grand piano is used to display the delicate conical arrangement, adding another feature to the far side of the room. Having a similar selection of flowers with a touch of pink freesia, the arrangement announces summer is really in the air.

THE PANEL ROOM

This room was originally part of the Great Hall but today it is used as a display area for the public. The panelling is of deal wood and has been grained to give the appearance of oak by the Victorian decorator, Williment, in 1839.

SIMPLY SPRING

The picture, plate and floral display make a delightful trio on the inlaid Hepplewhite bureau, which contains some intriguing love-letter hideaways and hidden drawers. Under the painting *Reflections* by Matthew Smith stands this delicate spring arrangement. Although this little arrangement is designed in a simple style it is very effective, and easy to accomplish.

To make a similar arrangement you need a small dish, one third of a brick of floral foam, tape, flowers and foliage to suit your own taste. When your mechanics are assembled, start by placing your foliage, using the euonymus to create your outline, together with eucalyptus and cornus. Flowers are then introduced one variety at a time, so you integrate the colour and shape of each flower evenly to make a balanced display. Place the longer stocks towards the top adding height, following the cream through the centre with primulas. Yellow heavily-scented *Mahonia aquifolium* tones beautifully with the variegated foliage; blue grey eucalyptus adds weight to the centre. Colour repeated in the *Muscari* and *Pulmonaria officinalis* can be found again in the painting.

FLOWERS
Peach *Chrysanthemum* (spray)
Primula vulgaris (polyanthus)
Pulmonaria officinalis (lungwort)
Muscari (grape hyacinth)
Mahonia aquifolium
Matthiola (stock)

FOLIAGE
Cytisus (broom)
Euonymus japonicus 'Ovatus Aureus'
Eucalyptus (gum tree)
Cornus alba 'Elegantissima' (dogwood)

FLOWERS AND FOLIAGE

Matthiola incana (stock)

Chrysanthemum 'Byoux'

Chrysanthemum 'Dramatic'

Gladiolus (sword lily)

Dianthus (orange carnation)

Dianthus (spray carnation)
Salix matsudana 'Tortuosa'

Eucalyptus (gum tree)

Aucuba japonica 'Variegata'

Tsuga (western hemlock or sugar pine)

Cytisus (broom)

A WARM GLOW

The thirteenth-century fireplace was replaced by the existing empire-style mantel shelf in 1839. Although this is a dark setting for flowers, the brilliant rust, orange and cream stand out beautifully from the rich panelling and fireplace surround, creating a warm glow, where a fire would normally burn brightly.

Salix matsudana 'tortuosa' winds its way through the flowers, adding a lighter texture, blending in with the accuba. Shafts of light draw attention to the pale cream scented stocks, accentuating a natural fall. A flat tray container with one brick of floral foam taped in has been used so that the arrangement stands steady and firm on the stone floor.

FOOT OF THE STAIRCASE
CASCADE

Under the painting of Katherine Countess of Rockingham, said to be by Van Loo in 1738, is a seventeenth-century Italian chest, upon which is displayed an arrangement of red lilies and gerberas depicting the colours of the full court regalia of the countess above. The colours also help to brighten and warm up the heavy, cold floors and walls.

This free-flowing design is full of interesting pieces of plant material differing in shape, colour and texture. All of these features add to the attractiveness of the display. Cystus spurts out like a fountain, changing this rather static triangle into a flowing form. The darker centres of the gerbera are repeated in the deep-grained wooden chest, their softer petal shades enhanced by the light streaming in from the open window nearby.

FLOWERS
Gerbera (Transvaal daisy)

Dianthus (spray carnation)

Lilium 'Red Night' (lily)

FOLIAGE
Sambucus racemosa 'Plumosa aurea' (golden elder)

Lonicera (honeysuckle)

Cornus alba 'Elegantissima' (dogwood)

Cytisus (broom)

Prunus laurocerasus (laurel)

Hedra helix (ivy)

SHUGBOROUGH

Nestling right in the Staffordshire countryside, a short distance from Stafford itself, the original house was built by William Anson in 1693 and later enlarged by his great grandson, Thomas, between 1745 and 1748. Thomas, founder member of the Dilettante Society and MP for Lichfield, extended the house, added the wings and commissioned the building of the temples and monuments in the park.

Samuel Wyatt was responsible for the last important additions to the mansion between 1790 and 1806, designed for Thomas's great nephew, 1st Viscount Anson.

The 5th Earl of Lichfield has established a reputation as one of the leading professional photographers of the day, under the name of Patrick Lichfield. He still continues to use part of Shugborough as his country home. In 1960 the Shugborough estate was given by the treasury to the National Trust and is now financed and administered by Staffordshire County Council. Today, David Hancock is the Director of Shugborough, responsible for the house and garden:

For all of us who have the privilege of working at Shugborough, the public enjoyment of the historic garden with its neo-classical monuments and the mansion house with its aura of Anson family history is paramount. It is vitally important for such a property to honour its own distinctive heritage, and to set its own style, never assuming, unwittingly, an alien National Trust identity. This precious individuality can be demonstrated very effectively through the medium of floral decorations in the house and in the character of the ornamental garden.

At Shugborough, despite being here nearly every day, I never get tired of the walk along the river towards the Chinese House, with its nearby red bridge and secretive island beyond. Each season displays new shades of old colours; it seems somehow to link the exploits of Admiral Anson two hundred and fifty years ago with the perceptive photographer's eye of the present Earl, Patrick Lichfield.

In the house, which is not too big to be a real family home, my favourite room is the Anson Room, which the public share with the family. Here the room is decorated to the taste of the family, who use it when Shugborough is closed to the public. So many historic houses reveal through their decoration the presence of a male administrator, lacking a lady's touch: flair, imagination and boldness. The Anson room features not ferns and ivies but spectacular lilies, colourful cyclamens and azaleas, huge but well-sited arrangements of cut or dried flowers. Its atmosphere is not that of frozen history but of a family home completed by the joy and subtlety of flowers, both inside and outside this historic place.

THE BLUE DRAWING ROOM
A PROFUSION OF PINK

This room, with its Chinese theme, was probably a dressing room in the late 1600s. The splendid marble chimney piece, thought to be by John Deval the Younger, was chosen as a background for this large yet soft and dainty arrangement. The unusual shade of blue lends itself to a contrasting shade of warm pinks.

FLOWERS
Chrysanthemum 'Lilac Byoux' (spray)
Paeonia officinalis (peony)
Pink *Dianthus* (perpetual-flowering carnation)
Dianthus (spray carnation)
Pink *Gladiolus* (sword lily)
Gypsophila paniculata (baby's breath)

FOLIAGE
Symphoricarpos albus (snowberry)
Fagus sylvatica 'Purpurea' (copper beech)

A fireplace is often a difficult area to decorate with flowers. It is important to keep your floral design within its contours, leaving any interesting detail on the surrounds still visible. A perfect base would be a large flat tray or dish filled with floral foam. Ensure your design remains firmly in place in it, though.

The clouds of soft gypsophila introduced sparingly amongst peonies, carnations, small spray carnations, gladioli and spray chrysanthemums create a large but delicate arrangement. You can see how by using an abundance of smaller-headed flowers, a lavish design can still be as effective as it would be if larger blooms were used.

THE RED DRAWING ROOM

This impressive room was created by Samuel Wyatt in 1794. The beautiful decorated plasterwork ceiling was by Joseph Rose the Younger, while the elegant white marble chimney piece was supplied by Richard Westmacott the Younger.

A Profusion of Pink in the Blue Drawing Room (above), and the Red Drawing Room (right) Shugborough

FLORAL CASCADE

The salmon-red room with its palest blue and gold ceiling lends itself to the richness of royal blue iris and delphiniums, complemented by creamy white carnations, gladioli and spray chrysanthemums. The unusual green seedheads come from the angelica plant, and make a striking piece of flora.

This display is nearly 10 feet tall, the great height achieved by mounting tubes on canes filled with floral foam, which are then inserted into the foam filled bowl. Delphiniums and gladioli are placed in the tubes to increase the height.

FLOWERS
Chrysanthemum (spray)
Dianthus (perpetual-flowering carnation)
Iris 'Professor Blaauw'
Gypsophila paniculata (baby's breath)

FOLIAGE
Fagus sylvatica (beech)
Angelica archangelica
Quercus robur (oak)

FLOWERS

Lilium 'Red Night' (lily)

Gladiolus (sword lily)

Alstroemeria (Peruvian lily)

Dianthus (spray carnation)

Gerbera 'Terramix' (Transvaal daisy)

Dianthus 'Harvest Moon' and orange carnation

FOLIAGE

Quercus robur (oak)

Ligustrum ovalifolium 'Aureum' (privet)

Fagus sylvatica 'Purpurea' (copper beech)

Cotinus coggygria 'Royal Purple' (smoke bush)

Prunus laurocerasus (laurel)

Fagus sylvatica (beech)

Cotoneaster

THE SALOON

In the days of Thomas Anson this room was used as the Dining Room, and in its original state was almost half its present length. Remodelled by Samuel Wyatt between 1803 and 1806, the length was extended, leaving the Saloon as we see it today.

AUTUMN GLOW

This display demonstrates how different varieties of foliage can be introduced to their best advantage: deep copper beech in a curved line through the arrangement picks up colour in the table; golden privet lightens the area slightly; and larger, heavier leaves of the oak add weight to the centre.

The gladioli lead the eye through the alstroemeria; orange lilies make way for the sunbursts of gerberas, and 'Harvest Moon' and tangerine carnations blend together, flowing gently in a natural fall over the table edge.

STANFORD HALL

Stanford Hall, a William and Mary house, was built in the 1690s for Sir Roger Cave by the Smiths of Warwick. It is the home of Lady Braye (who succeeded her Father in 1985) and her husband Lt Col. Aubrey-Fletcher. Lady Braye is a direct descendant of Sir Roger Cave. Stanford Hall in Leicestershire enjoys a peaceful view of the river Avon, which runs through the estate. Since succeeding to Stanford, Lady Braye has arranged all the flowers in the house herself, making full use of the lovely rose garden behind the Georgian stables.

The Ballroom, Stanford Hall

THE BALLROOM

This large Ballroom with its light and airy feel, is decorated in shades of soft peach and gold, and enjoys a south-facing aspect, ensuring a plentiful supply of natural light.

SUN BURST

This traditional, asymmetrical design, framed by the window recess, reveals the lawns and mature trees beyond. Gladioli accompanied by the dainty buds from spray carnations and chrysanthemums form the outline. Groupings of 'Doris' pinks fill in the centre, leaving the alstroemeria and lighter flowers back towards the outside. Gerberas resembling beautiful sun bursts glow warmly amongst the other flowers, and the completed bouquet suggests an old-fashioned garden on a hot summer's day, filled with colour and scent.

This large arrangement is displayed in a plastic bowl; floral foam is used and covered with chicken wire to give extra support. The whole assembly is then taped across the middle with floral sticky tape onto the bowl.

FLOWERS

Pink *Gladiolus* 'Friendship' (sword lily)

Alstroemeria (Peruvian lily)

Dianthus ('Doris' pink)

Pink *Dianthus* (spray carnation)

Chrysanthemum 'Refour'

Lilium 'Stirling Silver' (lily)

Gerbera 'Terramix' (Transvaal daisy)

FOLIAGE

Acuba japonica crotonifolia (spotted laurel)

Tsuga (western hemlock or sugar pine)

Arachniodes adiantiformis (leather fern)

Cupressus (cypress)

THE LIBRARY

Some 5000 books line the walls in this room and amongst them are papers and documents, mainly from Tudor, Jacobean and Georgian times; the oldest dated 1150, deals with a grant of Stanford land to Selby Abbey.

COMPLEMENTARY COLOURS

Assembled here for a striking red theme are shades of alstroemeria and whole and spray carnations, accompanied by sambucus with its striking yellow deeply indented foliage. Large hosta leaves of varying greens, a favourite with most flower arrangers, have also been introduced; their size adds weight to the base of the arrangement. Designed in a piece of floral foam taped into a small tray container, this floral piece suits the rich, sombre tones of the library. Although red is often a difficult colour to work with, the *Sambucus racemosa plumosa aurea* adds light and life to the whole, presenting a contrast to the leather-bound volumes beyond.

FLOWERS AND FOLIAGE
Alstroemeria (Peruvian lily)
Dianthus (red spray carnation)
Dianthus (perpetual-flowering carnation)
Hosta
Cotinus coggygria purpurea (smoke bush)
Cupressus (cypress)
Sambucus racemosa 'plumosa aurea'
Geranium foliage

THE GREEN DRAWING ROOM

This green panelled drawing room has a number of interesting paintings on show, including two by Van Dyck.

WHISPER OF DELIGHT

Delicate gypsophila sprays create a soft and pretty mist amongst the other pale flowers. These sprigs of tiny flowers are introduced sparingly, as the effect is far more subtle and natural than a fluffy cloud of gypsophila. A third of a brick of floral foam has been secured in the dish with sticky waterproof tape across the middle, leaving at least 7 cm (3 in) of foam above the sides.

White gladioli have been used for the three points, adding height and grace, and yellow alstroemeria, 'Fantasy' freesia and 'Stirling Silver' lilies give body to the display. Spray carnations create movement by curving softly in a line over to one side, away from the treasures on display, allowing the rich circular table to show through.

THE OLD DINING ROOM

These pictures, the old refectory table and the Charles II chairs came from the ancient house, which was pulled down when this one was built. The china displayed on the table is Royal Worcester.

Complementary Colours (left); Whisper of Delight (right); and Fruit and Flowers (below)

FLOWERS
Gladiolus (sword lily)
Cream *Chrysanthemum* (spider spray)
Alstroemeria (Peruvian lily)
Freesia 'Fantasy'
White *Dianthus* (spray carnation)
Lilium 'Stirling Silver'
Gypsophila paniculata (baby's breath)

FOLIAGE
Cornus alba 'spaethii' (dogwood)

FRUIT AND FLOWERS

To design this oval table-centre, the alstroemeria have been left long on their stems, together with pieces of foliage for length. Depth has been introduced by using lemon spider spray chrysanthemums, which takes the eye into the heart of the design; then roses, freesias and carnations are introduced. Finally, the artificial grapes are added, their dull gold glinting softly. On a table ladened with crackers, this would be a lovely centrepiece.

FLOWERS
Dianthus (cream carnation)
Chrysanthemum (spider spray)
Freesia
Alstroemeria (Peruvian lily)
Rosa 'Gerdo' (peach rose)

FOLIAGE
Cupressus
Hebe (veronica)
Tsuga (western hemlock or sugar pine)
Weigela 'Bristol Ruby'

STONELEIGH ABBEY

Stoneleigh Abbey stands in several acres of parkland near Kenilworth, in Warwickshire, close to the River Avon. Although deep in 'Shakespeare country', its roots go much further back to the twelfth century when, in 1154, Cistercian monks were granted the lands by Henry II.

The Dissolution of the Monasteries brought great change to Stoneleigh and it changed hands over several years, until bought by Sir Thomas Leigh and Sir Roland Hill jointly in 1561. The present Lord Leigh is a direct descendant of Sir Thomas Leigh, who cleared the ruins of the old Abbey and made it habitable once more. In the

House that stands today, Charles I was sheltered from Cromwell, and Queen Victoria stayed as a house guest.

Today, Stoneleigh is far more than just a grand residence. Its grounds are home to the National Agriculture Centre, and the Royal Show is held there annually. The gardens are tremendously important to the Leigh family, and Lady Leigh supervises the flowers for the main house:

It is impossible to live in the whole of Stoneleigh Abbey, which numbers over 150 rooms. Our State Rooms are used only occasionally by us and therefore lack that 'lived-in' feeling. Not wanting visitors to sense this, I have spent time leaving around half an unsmoked cigar, opened magazines, invitations on the mantle, dog baskets and well-chewed marrow bones on the Persian carpet in front of the fire in the Library. Family photographs, rumpled table napkins, half-filled decanters, gloves, fans and parasols all contribute, but the rooms only come alive when a clock chimes, a match is put to the logs and the flowers are arranged.

Planting with house-opening in mind includes varieties that can be dried, and we have many excellent dried flower arrangements throughout the house. In winter these are supplemented with very large arrangements of silk and even plastic flowers – now improved beyond all measure. A large flower bed containing only flowers to be used for cutting is vital to give fresh flowers from May to October. I include peonies, aquilegia, stocks, eryngium, Alchemilla mollis, *sweet peas, delphiniums, lupins, Iceland poppies, rudbeckia, dahlias, michaelmas daisies, and chrysanthemums. As well as all these, we have spring bulbs, flowering shrubs and evergreens. Unfortunately for the pocket a house with large scale rooms demands pot plants of a size far greater than is usually available locally. Dawn raids on the newly-sited London Flower Market at Nine Elms are well worthwhile for good'sized winter jasmine, lilies of all kinds, cymbidium orchids and great pots of hydrangeas.*

My personal passion is for old-fashioned roses which Peter Beales has supplied for the walled gardens at Stoneleigh. These are marvellous with the golds, pinks and whites of chrysanthemums, or with Cotoneaster horizontalis *with its pinkish-red foliage in autumn.*

THE SALOON

The elaborate plasterwork decorations and scagliola marble columns date from about 1765. The ceiling design depicts the apotheosis of Hercules in Olympus. This grand room is one of the finest examples of its type in the country. There are two full-length

portraits, one of Lady Caroline Leigh by Bardwell in 1753, and the second of Hélène, first wife of the third Lord Leigh, by E. Hughes.

EARLY AUTUMN

This wonderful light room with the grand piano at the far side and Regency breakfast tables, lends itself so well to floral displays. Using an autumn selection of chrysanthemum blooms and 'Charming' sprays intermingled with golden heads of solidago,

119

the whole area is lifted beautifully. This graceful form adopts a traditional style, with the gladioli adding height and width to one side as the piano narrows away. The carnations cascade gracefully over the edge of the dark wood to suggest airy movement. This selection of flowers would fit the occasion of a harvest supper, or even an Autumn wedding. Here, the colours blend well with the scagliola marble columns, which first inspired the design. The whole scene is completed by placing these small table posies on the two breakfast tables in the centre of the room. In these circular designs, flowers used in the piano arrangement have been repeated.

THE MONKS' UNDERCROFT

Traditionally, in a Cistercian abbey the undercroft was where the monks took their meals. An artist's impression of the Abbey when it was in full use in the thirteenth century, shows the kitchens leading out of the undercroft and the monks' dormitories on the floor immediately above. The dormitories would thus benefit from the kitchen heat, warming the sleeping quarters or at least alleviating the numbing cold. At Stoneleigh Abbey the Undercroft runs from north to south and has a stone-vaulted ceiling.

FLOWERS
Chrysanthemum 'Fred Shoesmith'
Chrysanthemum 'Cassandra' (bloom)
Gladiolus (sword lily)
Solidago (golden rod)
Chrysanthemum 'Charming' (spray)
Dianthus (perpetual-flowering carnation)

FOLIAGE
Weigela florida 'variegata'
Sambucus racemosa 'Plumosa Aurea'
(golden elder)

FLOWERS

Dianthus 'Mini Star' (orange spray carnation)

Dahlia

Gypsophila paniculata (baby's breath)

Rosa 'Belinda' (rose)

Chrysanthemum 'Charming' (spray)

Viburnum (red berries)

FOLIAGE

Hedera helix (ivy)

Fagus sylvatica (beech)

Early Autumn (left); Sunset (right); and the Monks' Undercroft, Stoneleigh Abbey (centre)

SUNSET

This room has an atmosphere of mystery surrounding it, created by the arched ceiling and grey sandstone walls, and here one can conjure up a sense of the Stoneleigh as mediaeval monastery without any difficulty.

With the help of reds and orange, this front-facing arrangement adds a bright splash of colour to an otherwise cool room. Rich red dahlias give impact, adding a stronger colour, whilst the rich orange spray chrysanthemums are placed informally throughout. Spray carnations curve outwardly with pieces of variegated ivy breaking up the outline. The roses are recessed slightly but stand out with their distinct petal formation. Viburnum berries, hanging in clusters, tone with the dahlias and successfully blend together in this simple bowl. By introducing small pieces of gypsophila, the stronger formation is broken slightly.

Flowers and natural stone make a change from the many varied settings encountered so far. These simple surroundings offer no complications with either choice of colours or style of design. A solid table deeply grained and unspoiled by varnish certainly helps to capture the aura of simplicity.

WARWICK CASTLE

Standing proudly overlooking the River Avon in the heart of the Midlands, Warwick is the finest example that survives of a mediaeval castle in Britain. Built by William the Conqueror in 1068, the Castle has passed down from Saxon earls to the present 37th Earl of Warwick, David Greville.

As a castle, Warwick contradicts all expectations – there are few cold, dark rooms or musty interiors in evidence. Instead, the overall impression is one of light surroundings, rich furnishings and an abundance of colours when you enter its sanctum.

FLOWERS AT WARWICK

By kind permission of Warwick Castle

It appears that flowers and various evergreens have been used to enhance the beauty of some of the rooms in the castle since the early part of the nineteenth century. For many years it was the responsibility of the head gardener not only to grow the required blooms, but also to arrange them.

In Victorian times, large palm trees in octagonal zinc-lined jardinières were an interesting and impressive contrast to the highly-polished glinting armour and weapons in the Great Hall.

The two principal State Rooms, in addition to the Great Hall, were the State Dining Room and the beautiful Cedar Drawing Room; these rooms were invariably heavily decorated with flowers – in jardinières, in large porcelain bowls and very tall fluted glass vases.

Amongst the most popular flowers were: rhododendrons, arum lilies, magnolias, dahlias, narcissi, gladioli, tulips, daffodils, and irises, accompanied by the appropriate greenery. On the more important religious feast days, Easter Sunday, All Saints and Christmas Day, flowers decorated the altar and the pulpit of the small family chapel.

Today, flower arrangements are the usual practice for the more important banquets, dinners and social evenings in the Great Hall and State Dining Room. Such arrangements vary of course according to the seasons of the year.

In the past all the evergreens and the flowers were, of course, grown in the castle grounds, in the conservatory, in the rose garden and in the glass or hot-houses. Today this is not the case, all such flower arrangements are ordered from an outside florist, but it is hoped that one day flowers and evergreens may be grown again in the castle grounds for room decoration.

Warwick Castle

THE STATE DINING ROOM

The new dining room was designed by Thomas Lightoler for Francis Greville, Earl of Warwick in 1763. Many craftsmen were involved in this extension to the Castle: the main structure was done by Job Collins and Thomas Briscoe, and the extensive wall panelling was the work of William Hands. This beautiful, gilded ceiling in the Jacobean style was by Robert Moore.

Hanging above the Adam fireplace, is an impressive picture of two lions, painted by Frans Snyders, who worked with Sir Peter Paul Rubens (1577–1640) at his studio. Dominating the room, is a magnificent painting of Charles I on his master horse, from Sir Anthony Van Dyck's studio (1599–1641). Other pictures include

those by Jonathan Richardson of Frederick, Prince of Wales (dated 1736), and work by the artist Charles Philips. The dining table is Victorian and around the room are six Venetian walnut parcel gilt armchairs by Brustolon, dated 1690; other chairs are eighteenth-century English.

Many distinguished guests have dined around this table including George IV, Queen Adelaide and Edward VII, and in 1858 Queen Victoria and Prince Albert had lunch here.

GOLDEN GLORY

The warm gold surroundings of such a rich setting can only enhance flowers. The arrangement in the centre of this table is in a long and low style, using a deep bowl filled with floral foam. The eremurus give height and length to the design and alstroemeria and off-white chrysanthemum blooms are placed across diagonally for width.

These beautiful, full, golden lilies are used to their best advantage, revealing rich brown stamens in the centres. Gypsophila just lightens the area slightly to soften the final look.

If you are attempting a large centrepiece, make sure that your arrangement is not too wide and does not get entangled with the table settings and wine glasses.

THE GREAT HALL

This room, built in the fourteenth century, would originally have had a large fire burning in its centre; a hole in the roof would have allowed the smoke to escape; and little narrow slits in the walls would have let through the light. Today the huge bay windows make the aspect much lighter but there is still a hint of the past.

When the hall was very badly damaged in 1871 by fire, a new roof was constructed and the Venetian marble floor relaid. In addition, a fireplace was installed to house the great log fires, which burnt daily, and the centre chandelier with its six lamps was added. All this renovation work was completed by Anthony Salvin in 1875.

On display in this room is a fine collection of armour and weapons, including a horse wearing equestrian armour. This room is the largest in the castle. It has a height of 40 feet, a length of 62 feet, and is 45 feet in width.

FLOWERS
Eremurus stenophyllus (foxtail lily)
Freesia
Chrysanthemum (bloom)
Lilium 'Connecticut King' (lily)
Chrysanthemum (spider spray)
Gypsophila paniculata (baby's breath)
Dianthus 'Candy White' (perpetual-flowering carnation)

FOLIAGE
Sorbaria arborea
Prunus laurocerasus (common laurel)
Cupressus (cypress)
Skimmia japonica

FIRE AND WAR

Golden Glory

A nineteenth-century buffet made in Kenilworth makes a beautiful backcloth for this arrangement. Deep peach chrysanthemums and red lilies give an autumnal feel, whilst also creating an atmosphere of great warmth.

The arrangement is designed as a conventional front-facing piece and still very effectively allows most of the rich carvings to remain visible. The solid piece of furniture was made in 1851, with deep chestnut colouring, which is found again in the red lilies, a focal point of this arrangement. Large chrysanthemum blooms give a more solid form, in keeping with the sturdy surrounds. A single flat tray with one and a half bricks of floral foam was used as a base for this display.

Fire and War

FLOWERS

Chrysanthemum (spider spray)

Lilium (red lily)

Achillea ptarmica 'The Pearl'

Dianthus (white spray carnation)

Limonium sinuatum (statice)

Dianthus (perpetual-flowering carnation)

Asparagus setaceus (fern)

Danae racemosa (ruscus)

Cornus alba elegantissima (dogwood)

Chrysanthemum 'Peach Mayford' (bloom)

FLOWERS

Chrysanthemum (thread -petalled spider spray)

Ornithogalum thyroides (chincherinchee)

Achillea ptarmica 'The Pearl'

Lilium 'Enchantment' (lily)

Dianthus (perpetual-flowering carnation)

Chrysanthemum 'Mayford' (bloom)

FOLIAGE

Asparagus setaceus (fern)

Cornus alba elegantissima (dogwood)

A Knight in Shining Armour

A Knight in Shining Armour

Arched stained-glass windows allow the light to stream through onto this effective table arrangement. The silhouette of the knight in shining armour, standing guard in the background, adds that authentic feel to life in a castle.

A matching selection of flowers to those used in the facing arrangement have been used once again, thus maintaining a classic continuity throughout the room. Chrysanthemum blooms add extra stability with their strong bold shape, and the carnations have been encouraged to fall naturally onto the table, whilst the spider-spray chrysanthemums are recessed.

Creamy-white chincherinchees together with achillea are dotted around the heavier flowers, sweeping around the candle in a graceful line across the centre. When using a candle in your display, leave a space in the middle of the flowers and foliage to eliminate any possible danger of a fire.

THE CEDAR DRAWING ROOM

Gold, heavy rich reds and pinks make up the grand decorations of the Cedar Drawing Room. The walls are panelled with a shining red-brown cedarwood, beautifully carved in the 1670s.

This heavily elaborate ceiling is about 300 years old and was designed by an English craftsman. A Waterford crystal chandelier from Ireland sparkles in the centre of the room. The nineteenth-century French carpet was woven in one piece, and incorporated in its corners is the Warwick Bear and Ragged Staff, along with the crest of the Greville family.

BAROQUE EXTRAVAGANCE

The flowers, here, stand on a fascinating Italian table, the top of which has an intricate design of marble inlaid with semi-precious stones and various marbles. This fountain of flowers is influenced by the way the creamy-white spider-spray chrysanthemums flow from the top through to the base of this design. It made a change to use a light contrast to relieve the strong, complicated surroundings. Cream in the alstroemeria and spider chrysanthemums is reflected in the fine Adam fireplace beyond. Spider blooms bursting out from amidst the other flowers, like excited

The Cedar Drawing Room, Warwick Castle

BAROQUE EXTRAVAGANCE

Catharine wheels, leave the curving stems of alstroemeria to dictate the outline, and the pink gerberas add necessary weight.

FLOWERS AND FOLIAGE

Gerbera (Transvaal daisy)

Achillea ptarmica 'The Pearl'

Chrysanthemum (thread-petalled spider spray)

Alstroemeria 'Mona Lisa' (Peruvian lily)

Arachniodes adiantiformis (leather fern)

Cotinus coggygria purpurea (smoke bush)

THE BLUE BOUDOIR

With blue silk-covered walls and an abundance of gold decorations, this small, cosy room houses a large portrait of Henry VIII after the style of the great Hans Holbein, and Louis XVI furniture which has been here since the 1870s.

CLASSIC SIMPLICITY

Cascading blue cornflowers, spray carnations and chincherinchees make up part of this design, continuing the startling blue colour theme. A gilded female figure is the base of this delicate Venetian console table which proudly supports the display. To add informality and freshness to an otherwise classic design, it is important to suggest movement in the flowers – tiny blue powder puffs are casually intermingled with tumbling white gem stones and ivy skeins twist and turn through the arrangement.

FLOWERS AND FOLIAGE

Centaurea cyanus (cornflower)

Limonium sinuatum (statice)

Achillea ptarmica 'The Pearl'

Ornithogalum thyrsoides (chincherinchee)

Dianthus (spray carnation)

Hedra helix 'Glacier' (ivy)

Hebe (veronica)

Spiraea × *arguta*

132

WESTON PARK

Weston Park is a magnificent seven-teenth-century mansion house set in the county of Shropshire. Famous for its extensive Capability Brown parkland, it has been the ancestoral home of the earls of Bradford for 300 years. The main entrance and doorway were originally on the south side of the house, but the 3rd Earl of Bradford moved them to where the library stood in the nineteenth century.

THE ENTRANCE HALL

A soft, delicate shade of green covers the wall and gold leaf picks out the neat detail on the frieze and columns in the entrance hall. The horse paintings by Stubbs, E M Fox and John Ferneley bedeck the walls, imparting an air of grandeur and aloofness.

MEMORIES

Because of the formality of this room, a soft yet striking design seems most appropriate. A simple selection of roses and carnations are used as a source of strong pink, but softened with hosta and helleborus, in toning shades of apple green. The shape is allowed to flow and trickle lazily over the edge of the French writing table, and the deep pink flowers are set off by the pale background.

THE TAPESTRY ROOM

The tapestry room has a crushed, raspberry-pink glow with garlands of flowers draped across the top edge of each exquisite tapestry, of which there are only six similar sets left in existence

The Entrance Hall, Weston Park (above);
and Memories (opposite)

FLOWERS
Dianthus (pink spray carnation)
Dianthus (carnation)
Helleborus corsicus

FOLIAGE
Buxus sempervirens (box)
Taxus baccata (yew)
Fagus sylvaticus (beech)
Weigela variegata
Hosta (plantain lily)
Rosmarinus officinalis (rosemary)

today. They were commissioned by the first Bridgeman owner of
Weston, Sir Henry and woven at the famous Gobelin factory in
Paris.

SPECIAL CELEBRATION

The dark leather top of the Louis XV Kingswood writing table is
a perfect position for this arrangement. The display takes the
shape of a cross, allowing the flowers to flow softly between the
delicate ornaments and photographs on display, and matches the

The Tapestry Room, Weston Park (left); and
Special Celebration (above)

romantic design of the French furniture. Designed in a long flat tray with two thirds of a brick of foam, the space available on the desk was measured carefully before the arrangement was started.

'Bridal Pink' roses, spray and large carnations in a delicate pink lift the design away from the writing desk. The light and airy appearance is changed dramatically when the deep blue 'Professor Blaauw' irises are added, their colour repeated in the treasurers on display. The overall mood is then lightened by elaeagnus, used on the reversed side to show its silver-grey leaves, and the spider-spray chrysanthemums with their spiky petal formation give an oriental look, linking up with the table lamps behind.

FLOWERS
Rosa 'Bridal Pink' (rose)

Dianthus 'Hellas' (carnation)

Dianthus (spray carnation)

Iris 'Professor Blaauw'

FOLIAGE
Cotoneaster × *Hybridus-pendulus*

Elaeagnus ebbingei

Taxus baccata (yew)

Tsuga (western hemlock or sugar pine)

THE DRAWING ROOM
The Drawing Room has many important portraits displayed within, one of which is of Lady Wilbraham by Sir Peter Lely. She married Sir Thomas Wilbraham in 1651 at Weston and began to rebuild the house and stable in 1671.

ALL ON A SUMMER'S DAY
Surrounded by family photographs, this glorious summer display with gilded foliage reflects with the gold edging on the Louis XV desk. By simply using gold spray paint on selected pieces of foliage, a similar effect is created. As you can see, the foliage has

All on a Summer's Day

been inserted sparingly amongst the orange and yellow flowers, the variegated elaeagnus toning nicely with the pale green euphorbia. Golden sharon fern falls vertically from both sides, and larger golden laurel leaves shimmer as the light catches them. The eye is led into the arrangement down the left side by deep tangerine carnations balanced on the right-hand side with yellow freesia and 'Refour' chrysanthemum spray.

THE DINING ROOM

Chandeliers, heavy gilt frames, flower garlands and ceiling moulds touched with gold complete the splendour of the grand dining room. The oak panelling, which once decorated the walls, can

FLOWERS

Chrysanthemum 'Refour'

Alstroemeria (Peruvian lily)

Dianthus 'Raggio di Sole' (carnation)

Lilium 'Enchantment' (lily)

Freesia (gold)

FOLIAGE

Prunus laurocerasus (common laurel)

Hedera helix (ivy)

Elaeagnus pungens maculata

Euphorbia polychroma (spurge)

Nephrolepis exaltata (Boston fern)

now be found in Finchingfield Church in Essex. The wallpaper of Italian design was commissioned by the late Lady Mary Bradford and she supervised its manufacture in the factory in north London.

FLOWERS BY CANDLELIGHT

These two centrepieces were made to match as closely as possible, which can be quite a difficult task, especially when arrangements are to be displayed so closely together. The best way to achieve this, however, is to get both containers, 'greened' with foliage to the same stage, then introduce flowers for the length, alternating as you go. Smaller, dainty heads are used around the edge to create your outline, and flowers placed across the centre add a little height. Blooms in a deeper shade are used in recess; the roses left on longer stems then become the more important flower. Ensure you view each piece from all angles; if anything appears out of line, minor adjustments can now be made.

Flowers by Candlelight

FLOWERS
Rosa 'Gerdo' (rose)
Alstroemeria (Peruvian lily)
Lathyrus odoratus (sweet pea)
Dianthus (spray carnation)
Matthiola incana (stock)
Freesia

FOLIAGE
Berberis darwinii (barberry)
Vinca (periwinkle)
Hosta (plantain lily)
Weigela 'variegata'
Skimmia japonica
Tsuga (western hemlock or sugar pine)
Euonymus

Deep crushed raspberry-pink alstroemeria has been used, which tones with the rich wall colouring. Perfume lingering lightly in the air from the sweet peas, roses and freesia, which make up the body of these displays, makes the arrangement particularly attractive for a dinner party when your guests are close enough to the flowers to appreciate their fragrance. When designing dinner table centre-pieces, try to add flowers with a gentle aroma, as this helps to create a relaxed atmosphere. By introducing cream and white a further link with the surrounding dado and fireplace has been made to integrate the flowers and decor.

Remember to remove flowers from polished surfaces before attempting to water them as water droplets can mark wood easily.

THE SECOND SALOON

The second saloon was originally the smoking room leading off the billiard room. Displayed in the cabinets is a rare and valuable collection of illustrated bird books by Gould, published between 1832 and 1861. The striking black and white floor was laid to match the marble in the hall, and was put down in 1960 after the oak floor was found to be riddled with furniture beetle.

TOUCH OF MAGIC

A striking arrangement stands gracefully in the centre of a very bold room, dominated by these black slate and white marble tiles. Glowing red gladioli, gerbera and freesia threaded like rubies through cream lilies, stocks and spider-spray chrysanthemums. Golden-sprayed fern leaves shimmer as they reflect the light streaming down from above, adding a touch of splendour – it makes the whole concept that much more interesting if you can conceal one or two hidden surprises, for instance gilded foliage, berries, nuts or pieces of driftwood.

Cascading leaves of forsythia, weigela and Solomon's seal creating a natural curve at the base of the design, and the straight sword-like gladioli take the eye up towards the light and away from the dramatic tile formation.

THE BREAKFAST ROOM

This room houses a special collection of small portraits, and for this purpose special picture lighting has been installed. One of the most important pictures in the house is displayed here, a portrait

FLOWERS
Gladiolus (sword lily)
Lilium 'Sterling Star' (lily)
Gerbera (Transvaal daisy)
Matthiola (stock)
Syringa (common lilac)
Freesia 'Oberon'
Chrysanthemum (cream spider spray)

FOLIAGE
Euonymus
Hosta (plantain lily)
Arachniodes adiantiformis (leather fern)
Hedera helix (ivy)
Cornus alba 'Elegantissima' (dogwood)
Forsythia (golden bells)

...of Sir George Grove by Holbein, the drawing of which is at Windsor Castle. The late eighteenth century shield-back chairs around the room are by Hepplewhite.

GARDEN PARADISE

The paradise design includes sweet peas, Solomon's seal and a rose called 'La Minuette', and the colours pick up the red damask wallcovering. What could be better than roses and sweet peas placed together in a group of similar colours and... Wonderful scents and textures combined together will suit any theme. Just alter the arrangement to suit the space you have available.